Günter Grass

Modern Literature Monographs

Günter Grass

KURT LOTHAR TANK

Translated by JOHN CONWAY

Frederick Ungar Publishing Co.
New York

Translated from the German *Günter Grass* by special arrangement with the original publisher, Colloquium Verlag, Berlin

Contents

1

Live
with Matzerath?

"**A**t last German postwar literature has its young lion: Günter Grass." The critic was Arthur Lundkvist, writing in the *Stockholms Tidningen* on October 16, 1961. Some days later these words appeared in the Paris *Carrefour*: "French novelists, veil your heads! If there were a European tournament of novelists, you would be bested—last season by Lampedusa, and this season by somebody named Günter Grass."

A few weeks earlier, in the *France Observateur*, André Dalmas had declared:

If the reader really wants to compare the novel *The Tin Drum* with a literary work that he already knows, he would have to turn to Sterne's *Tristram Shandy* to be able to judge the multiplicity and power of the themes; the fascination of the blasphemous, the salaciousness or eroticism, the power and the humor appear in the course of the episodes together with the historical fidelity of this whole confusion of content. The story of Oskar, Günter Grass's hero, is the same kind of hybrid autobiography as that of Tristram Shandy.

This drummer, says the article, puts the entire world in motion.

Through creative imagination Oskar has been able to become the nucleus of a gigantic molecule, for it is through creative imagination that Oskar unveils the world at the same time that the world unveils itself. But the humor of this intimate language does not permit the reader to discover Oskar. Oskar does not exist, or rather, he exists only through the narrator, who awakes him to life. One never meets the author without his hero. They speak with each other and stick together. What the author cannot see, Oskar shows him. Where the author cannot go, Oskar leads him. When the author calms down, Oskar revolts. Oskar—the misshapen hero, a product of imagination who can be compared to an insect—with his language slowly destroys step by step the whole edifice that the narrator has built up in front of him.

One could cite hundreds of critiques from France and Scandinavia, England and the United States. Contradictory as they may be in interpretation, in the pros and cons of their evaluation, what remains indisputable is that Günter Grass has set the literary world in motion, in an uproar, with his drummer boy. Much of this partially scandal-enveloped sensation may have been induced by publicity ballyhoo and nonliterary motives and increased by fashion and the habit of "follow the leader." Nevertheless three things can clearly be seen: the originality, the literary rank, and the intellectual-sociological standpoint of Günter Grass. With Grass, German literature—after Benn and Brecht—has again made contact with world literature.

By struggle, by defiance—as it were, by beating the drum—Grass has won an area of freedom for the imagination and—with imagination's help—for the individual in society. Here anarchy stands against anarchy, the joy of individual destruction against state-directed power of destruction. In his 1964 essay "Avantgardismus und die Zukunft der modernen Kunst" [Avant-gardism and the Future of Modern Art], Hans Egon Holthusen defines this area of freedom more precisely. He stresses the power of the narrator, the vehement tale teller from the Langfuhr suburb of Danzig. It is significant when a leading German critic with a reputation for conservatism speaks of a reintegration of prose and asserts freely:

The Tin Drum restores the form of the novel, perhaps not once and for all, but still for this one time: the novel in its freshest, most entertaining, uninhibitedly anecdotal version, the novel as an adventurous sequence of picaresque stories.

And it is at least as significant when the respected German scholar and literary critic Anni Carlsson ranks Grass's second novel, *Dog Years,* highly. In an article in the *Neue Zürcher Zeitung* of November 21, 1964, entitled "Der Roman als Anschauungsform der Epoche/Bemerkungen zu Thomas Mann und Günter Grass [The Novel as the Expression of Outlook in Our Epoch: Observations on Thomas Mann and Günter Grass], she writes as follows:

It is particularly instructive to consider *Faustus* and *Dog Years* side by side as character displays of the same epoch. At first glance, the novel about a musician written by the septuagenarian citizen of the world from Lübeck has nothing in common with the Vistula epic written by the thirty-six-year-old native of Danzig. A closer look at the outlines of the two works, however, shows surprising analogies which perhaps suggest certain conclusions about the methods of that period in the writing of imaginary history.

At the close of her essay, a model study of comparative literature, Anni Carlsson writes that the epoch portrayed by Thomas Mann and Günter Grass is hellish.

But whereas in *Faustus* an infernal, long-inherited national sickness now enters its final stage, for Grass the "dog years" are an infernal episode. What remains behind is a burst and cloven postwar Germany, inhabited by scarecrows and covered with excrement. In it live—as a kind of counter-poison—the trio Walter, Jenny, and Goldmäulchen, whose essence is a bitter, crystalline artistic humanity. Resigned, with a laughing glance at the absurd world, the survivors praise the eternal flux of happening and of stories, lifting their glasses to it in a toast. Thomas Mann called *Faustus* his *Parsifal*. Walter Matern's notes in *Dog Years* are entitled "Materniads." Both *Faustus* and *Dog Years* employ a parody of the heroic poem to characterize an epoch. Thomas Mann's parody is ironic-elegiac in nature; that of Grass is satiric-elegiac, the elegiac climax being Jenny's toe dance in the snow. Doctor Faustus perishes with his epoch; Eddi Amsel and Walter Matern survive theirs.

In Oskar, the tin drummer, Günter Grass has succeeded in creating a peculiar and indeed original figure, at once very simple and highly complex. It is a figure which invites the most varied and contradictory interpretations—and yet which resists all interpretations, preserving its secret like a figure in a fairy tale while calling forth other figures from fairy tales and folk rhymes: a witch master whom the Black Cook of the nursery rhymes bewitches and dominates, who can shatter glass by singing and work wonders, wonders that we believe of him, that amaze or shock us a little, and which we cannot get enough of. We adults feel as if we were transported back to the days of our childhood, when with astonishment we shared Gulliver's and Robinson Crusoe's experiences with them. But at the same time we know that in this gnome Oskar has been conjured up the spirit and demon of an epoch—howling lasciviousness, malice, blasphemy. His is an infantilism that suddenly assumes demonic shape, that is, ethically uncontrolled yet acts with deadly certainty of purpose, at the same time appearing almost innocent, fleeing into hiding places, seeking shelter under grandmother's wide skirts, using reactions compounded of cruelty and innocence to shut itself off from the unholy adult world.

Whereas German reviewers—even Günter Blöcker, for example—accentuate the antihumane character of *The Tin Drum* and its narrator-hero, most of the French critics emphasize different aspects of the work. Besides comparing it with the world of the Germanic sagas and Hieronymus Bosch's world of images, they relate it to contemporary history and also stress—astonishingly—the book's moral tendency. Thus Henri Petit, writing in the *Parisien libéré* of October 31, 1961, made this evaluation:

Günter Grass has his own way of setting a world in motion while preserving a singular intellectual freedom throughout an entire population of characters that is portrayed at once satirically and symbolically. His drum-beating hero is a dwarf, a dwarf of his own free will who for a number of reasons did not want to grow bigger. The best of it is that he wanted to preserve the mad independence of an evil spirit in order to further examine what lies behind things. Tirelessly he explains to us fifty years of Germany's history. A giant could not have brought that feat off; he would have stumbled over his legs, his arms, his brain, and his pen.

This remark, at once penetrating and helpful, reveals *The Tin Drum*'s substratum and its secret dialectic. To reach this value-free position, which is not without its dangers. Günter Grass and his hero and monster Oskar Matzerath had to pay a fairly high price: they had to identify themselves with evil. They had to do this in order to overcome guilt—a new and vicious guilt—and the poison of self-righteousness. Another and older, more profound critic of Germany, Thomas Mann, drew close to this delicate problem in a similar manner. One of his strangest writings is a little-known work that bears the title *Bruder Hitler* [Brother Hitler].

To speak plainly, Oskar Matzerath is a part of us Germans just as Adolf Hitler is a part of us and our history. Like Hitler (and the "Hitler in us"), the tin drummer Oskar Matzerath who is around us and in us is something we must also overcome. Our involvement in guilt cannot be canceled by shunting it aside or by a pharisaical defamation of Günter Grass. Neither can it, for that matter, be eliminated by limiting ourselves to aesthetic and ethical evaluation nor by taking an intellectual or sociological point of view of the work. One of the best and most valuable things about the book is that it arouses a strong and long-lasting disquiet.

Files could be filled with the utterances of readers who have felt shocked and outraged by *The Tin Drum*. This fact is attested to by letters to newspapers, to Grass himself, and to critics who have dared to comment favorably on his book. It is striking that readers whose spelling is unobjectionable— even men with doctoral degrees, professors, and senate presidents—are stimulated by Günter Grass to use plain language of a sort not ordinarily found in readers' letters. One other observation seems significant to me. Although positive and negative judgments regarding the book are to be met with among young as well as older readers, among the youth— with individual exceptions—a greater absence of bias, a greater readiness to examine Grass's criticism of society, including those passages of the book which have been termed offensive or shocking, can be seen.

Borchert and Böll, who were much read after 1945, scored their successes primarily with their short stories and satires. Günter Grass is the first to succeed in making postwar German literature so interesting to large numbers of people in Germany and abroad, and especially to young people in Germany, that they plunge into the adventure of reading an (in part) exacting and tedious book of 734 pages with eagerness and inner sympathy. *The Tin Drum,* which five years after its appearance had run to 500,000 copies in Germany alone, is actually read line by line. So are the novella *Cat and Mouse* (which like *The Tin Drum* has been put out in Germany in a paperback edition) and the thick novel *Dog Years.* And these books are eagerly discussed, above all by high school, technical school, and university students. The discussions are by no means always favorable. The young people have a very good critical sense and are without snobbery.

Most of them see very clearly what distinguishes Grass from many other novelists. He does not treat the problems of the individual and society on the level of current judgments and prejudices. He goes into the substratum of existence, and out of the insecurity of an agitated age he builds up a (highly dubious) picture of mankind. He offers us no tragic heroes or positive heroes, as the epoch of German idealism did and as the doctrine of socialist realism requires.

Even if one wished to see only a fool in Oskar, one should still recognize that in foolish times this fool fulfills a function which preacher and pedagogue often fail in because they do not reach each man and appeal to him where such an appeal should be made: to his subconscious, to his dreams. What takes place in *The Tin Drum*, and also in *Cat and Mouse* and *Dog Years,* is a process—a process of the imagination into which every reader is drawn, willingly or unwillingly. Originally a figment of the author's imagination, a vital figure such as the tin drummer Oskar gains power over us; his demonic powers awaken other powers in us, affirmative and defensive powers that make us capable of self-assertion in a new area of freedom that is not without danger, and always in danger. Such a figure, whether he be called a negative hero or a fool, has substance and creates substance. Through such a figure, greater depths of the soul are reached; that which once was, becomes alive; sunken and forgotten images, sagas, fairy tales, and myths enter our consciousness anew. And these older, deeper, ineradicable reserves become the standard for estimating the worth of the new.

Of the external facts of Günter Grass's life little needs to be said and known. He was born in the Langfuhr suburb of Danzig on October 16, 1927, the son of German-Polish parents. As a boy he met with Germans and Poles, Cassubians, and gypsies in towns and villages at the mouth of the Vistula. At the age of seventeen he was drafted into the infantry. On April 20, 1945, he was wounded at Cottbus.

After release from an American prisoner-of-war
camp in 1946, he did temporary work on a farm
and in a potash mine. In the following years he
learned sculpture in a stonemason's workshop and
at the Kunstakademie in Düsseldorf. Later, in Berlin, he was a pupil of Karl Hartung. In between he
worked as a jazz musician and on a dance stage. He
wrote poems and plays. In 1958 he received the
prize of the Gruppe 47; in 1960, the Berlin Critics'
Prize; in 1962, the Paris Prix du Meilleur Livre
Étranger (for *The Tin Drum*). Grass is married. He
has four children and lives in Berlin.

In a conversation with Horst Bienek, Günter
Grass has said that his native city of Danzig and the
suburb of Langfuhr are for him the capital, the center, of the world, and that all other German cities
—Düsseldorf, Hamburg, Cologne, Berlin—are only
suburbs of this central point, around which everything that moves him and the world still revolves
today. In actual fact, without Danzig and the lowland of the Vistula the literary work of Günter
Grass is unthinkable. Many of his poems, some
scenes of his plays, and, above all, the novels and
the novella *Cat and Mouse* receive their color, individuality, and contours from the experiences of his
childhood and youth.

Günter Grass, fundamentally, develops few
themes. They form a texture, or—more precisely—
a pattern. It is the pattern of a modern mythology
which despite—or indeed because of—its reversion
to archaic or archetypical elements depends upon a
new experience of reality. It would be premature

today to examine in detail the origin of this world of myth, the linking and altering of these themes, and Grass's continually fresh examination, intensification, and mutation of them. Grass stands not at the end but at the beginning, or perhaps at the mid-point, of a line of development that still leaves much to be determined. In any case it will be well to use the simple basic elements of his work as a point of departure. They are best surveyed where they are found in their purest state, in his lyric poetry. Beginning with the lyrics and continuing with a critical analysis of his dramatic works, our approach will lead us to the complex forms, his two novels *The Tin Drum* and *Dog Years.* Together with the novella *Cat and Mouse,* they form at once a self-contained edifice and yet a foundation completely capable of further development. The foundation consists of *petit bourgeois* houses, bunkers, and half-sunken wrecks, underground factories, human beings and beasts, and a variety of museum pieces. At the end of *Dog Years* the manufacturer Brauxel —who was once called Eduard Amsel and then Goldmäulchen—places the dog Pluto, once called Prinz, at the entrance to the underground factory. He chains the black shepherd dog to his place and says:

What object worth guarding has the cheerful daylight surface of the earth to offer a dog such as this? Here is his place. Here, where the mine shaft says Amen and there is piped down from above the fresh air of May. He shall be guardian here and yet he shall not be called Cerberus. Orcus is up above.

2

Diana,
or the Objects

Günter Grass made his entry into German literature very quietly, almost unnoticed. The year was
1956, and his first book was a volume of lyrics and
short prose pieces. Beasts that the author drew in
stilted postures, craning their necks, crowing, cack-
ling, surround a title that seems hovering between
sand and sky: *Die Vorzüge der Windhühner* [The
Merits of Windfowl]. In a poem printed on the dust
jacket in the place where the blurb normally appears,
Grass explains his sympathy for the creatures of a surrealistic imagination.

Because they take up hardly any room
On their perch made of an air draft
And do not peck at my tame chairs.
Because they do not disdain the hard rind of dreams,
Nor run after the letters of the alphabet
That the postman loses every morning in front of my door.
Because they remain standing,
From the breast to the tail
A patient surface covered with very small writing,
With not a quill nor apostrophe forgotten . . .
Because they leave the door open
To which the key is allegory,
Which crows now and then.
Because their eggs are so light
And digestible, and transparent.
Who saw this moment
When the yellow has enough, pricks up its ears and falls
    silent?
Because this quiet is so soft,
The flesh on the chin of a Venus,
I nourish it.—
Often when the east wind blows,
Riffling the partitions like pages of a book,
They open to a new chapter.

> Then I lean happily on the fence,
> Without having to count the fowls—
> Because they are numberless and steadily increasing.

One thinks of Paul Klee when one takes these and other lines in this volume of poetry and, instead of actually reading them, visualizes them. One feels with tender fervor the gaiety, light as a dream, with which the poet nourishes the windfowls of his own invention that lend wings to his creative act. Veiled references are everywhere: to banal, useless colloquial speech (the letters of the alphabet lost by the postman); to the meaning that has become a cliché (the key, allegory, which the dictionary defines as "in art, a representation of abstract concepts that endows them with life."). With shattering comedy, the abstract concept in the poem becomes itself endowed with life: it crows. That which has been talked to death it crows back to life again, gives nonsense a "knock on the head," makes knife, fork, shears, and light play absurd games, sees "the air full of shears" and the sky as a pattern. On the gas storage tank of the suburban town is set a toad:

> It breathes in and out
> So that we can cook.

Playfully and precisely, Grass's fancy sees himself and his position in the quatrain "Nächtliches Stadion" [Stadium at Night]:

> Slowly the football rose in the sky.
> Now one could see that the stands were filled.
> Alone the poet stood as goalkeeper,
> But the referee whistled: "Off side."

When Günter Grass published these and other verses in his first volume of poetry—as a basis for a new creative picture of the world—the literary referees did not blow the whistle. They received the inconspicuous gray volume without surprise. Perhaps they read the brief notice of the publisher, Luchterhand Verlag: "Günter Grass was born in 1927 in Danzig, and studied to be a sculptor in Düsseldorf. A pupil of Karl Hartung, he has worked in Berlin since 1953 as a sculptor, illustrator, and writer." Perhaps the literary referees regarded with more amusement than enthusiasm the remarkable, sometimes obscure drawings by Grass that were added to the slender volume: beasts of fable in stilted attitudes, strange objects, and fairy-tale motifs, a broad expressionistic hand with six fingers, and sharp shears that cut the pattern of the sky to ribbons.

What was thought of the poems? Probably not too much. In a lyric poetry contest the South German Radio Network had given Günter Grass third prize. Of course even at a cursory glance it was hardly possible to overlook his originality and inventiveness and the precision of his images. Here were acute aphorisms and new formulations, a humor that dug traps, and, above all, a gift that had not appeared for a long time in such elemental form: the gift of conveying plot with the poem, sufficient plot for a story, a drama, a novel. Sometimes a grotesque scene lingered in the memory, as in the poem "Die Schule der Tenöre" [The School for Tenors]:

> How beautifully Else Fenske sang
> When, in the summer vacation,
> At a great height she missed a step,

> Plunged into a silent glacier's crevasse,
> And left behind only her little parasol
> And the high C.

Assaults, attempted murders, and sinister everyday scenes in which the present becomes senseless in view of a murdered future—this is what leaps out at us from five lines written in the shorthand of a black humor that contains more than the marketable kind of social criticism. The poem is entitled "Familiar" [Family Affairs]:

> In our museum—we go there every Sunday—
> They have opened a new department.
> Our aborted children, pale, serious embryos,
> Sit there in plain glass jars
> And worry about their parents' future.

That sounds like a brief roll of the tin drum. In actual fact we find in the not quite fifty pages of this volume of lyrics many themes that forecast later works: novels, stories, and plays. Such motifs are sounded in the poems that make up "Der elfte Finger" [The Eleventh Finger], in the cycle "Drei Vater Unser" [Three Our Fathers], and in the verses entitled "Polnische Fahne" [Polish Banner]. There we read the short poem out of which Grass has built a two-act play; the poem and the play alike are entitled *Hochwasser* [The Flood]. In illustrations and in poems there emerges vividly a major theme of his novel *Dog Years*: human beings in the form of birds and scarecrows. The first poem in the first volume of lyrics bears the title "Vogelflug" [Bird Flight]. Another short poem, "Musik im Freien" [Open-Air Music], closes with the lines:

When the yellow dog ran over the meadow
The concert died.
Later the bone could not be found.
The notes lay under the chairs,
The conductor lifted his airgun
And shot all the blackbirds.

Anyone who has read the novel *Dog Years* will not be able to regard these verses as a detached sort of surrealistic or absurd playfulness, but rather as an attempt to capture the horrors of experienced reality in images that are at once familiar and strange. The fable of the five birds which Grass relates in his first volume of poetry is also strangely rich in mental associations. At the end the birds are going to "lay and hatch five eggs, one for each continent. Who knows all that lies between egg white and egg yolk? In any case the eggs are to be full of impressive surprises for Europe, America, and the other continents." Poem V, "Der Vogel" [The Bird], seems like shorthand notes for the scarecrow theme which unfolds in full breadth in *Dog Years*.

Not all of the themes and motifs that are later developed in dramatic or epic form are successfully executed with such abundance and virtuosity as is the Matzerath cipher in the second of the "Drei Vater Unser":

Lack of fools, which still breeds humps . . .

And the chiming in at the beginning:

Force, which bent the safety pin,
Which gave cabbage-headed nonsense a knock on the head.
They simply come,
Shatter the glasses by singing,

> And still want applause.
> Mars, evil butchers, set the prices.

What arises in earlier verses out of the depth of a childhood enveloped in magic, experienced with a rounded sensuousness and a glaring vividness that is demonic, takes on, in metaphors and ciphers, the first outline of a mythology that is at once archetypical and individual. And it will find its outlet again and again in new literary creations—lyric, epic, dramatic—and in illustrations and sculpture. There will be *one* preponderant theme: the Langfuhr area of Danzig and the Vistula lowland, and their peoples, in response and in resistance, extending like survivals of earlier times into this age of technology and total war that is continued in still untested forms—an open-ended process whose perspective Gottfried Benn has hinted at in his posthumous essay "Der Radardenker" [The Radar Thinker].

Will man be the victor once again? Is a new species of man coming? How strong are the rudiments of animism? Can they hold their own against technological reality? Or are they hopelessly inferior to it?

> You are to inoculate no more rats,
> You are to bury all towers,
> Our Father who art in heaven.

The entreating imperative—imperious, devout, or blasphemous—must be understood according to the rules of the game that is being played with and against the reader or spectator. Grass belongs to a generation that is like the burned child. Once before

in Germany there had been such a generation, after
World War I. At the time Ernst Glaeser wrote the
novel *Jahrgang 1902* [The 1902 Age Group]. The
1927 age group, to which Grass belonged, was the
same age when World War II began as the 1902
group had been at the outbreak of World War I.
Both groups' experience of life were similar: ration-
ing of food substitutes and substitutes for love. The
poem "Blechmusik" [Music for Brasses] describes the
arc that leads from the lived-out idyl of childhood to awareness of death,/ flight, and the grave,
back to the recollection of early childhood dreams
undisturbed by any warning signal:

> Back then we slept in a trumpet.
> It was very quiet there.
> We did not dream the trumpet would blow,
> And, as if in proof that it would not,
> We lay open-mouthed in its throat—
> Back then, before we were blown out.

Ernst Jünger speaks of the calm center of the
typhoon. It offers shelter against threatening storms;
in it the work of the writer grows and develops. The
continuing din that Günter Grass released in the fall
of 1959 with *The Tin Drum* drowned out the sound
of the lyrics born in the eye of the storm, in the core
of his being. The uproar was not a chance event.
Grass had provoked it, or—more precisely—had
had it provoked by a figure of his narrative art. This
character, who has since become a national figure, is
the dwarf Oskar Matzerath, nonhero, monster, a
malicious and blasphemous creature possessed of an
infantile cunning. As the novel begins, he is lying in

bed in a mental hospital. There, with the help of a tin drum from which he has never parted since his earliest years, he writes the memoirs—unbelievable and shocking, shameless and candid, in part repugnant—of thirty years of dissolute life in a no less dissolute epoch.

Günter Grass's drum-beating crank is the direct opposite of the best-selling author John Belitz, the opportunist who invariably offers his stellar performance under every regime, whom Heinz von Cramer introduced to readers in 1958 in a book entitled *Die Kunstfigur* [The Figure of Artifice]. Cramer's figure of artifice created no sensation. Günter Grass's elemental figure released an uproar that made itself heard far beyond the confines of the literary market. In the winter of 1959 the din reached a climax when the Senate of Bremen refused to give Grass the literature prize which a respected panel of judges had intended for him. In the years following, as the din died down, starting up again occasionally, Günter Grass became—if not a literary great—a figure with a recognized market value. Meanwhile further works of his have appeared in print: the plays *The Wicked Cooks* (1961) and *The Flood* (1963), the novella *Cat and Mouse* (1961), and the novel *Dog Years* (1963). Grass became a "man of prominence." But interesting as his increasing fame made the mustached man from Danzig-Langfuhr—his partiality to nuns, scarecrows, and the Social Democratic Party, his love of cooking ("I like to cook; for example, I enjoy cooking lentils"), his now fresh

and unbiased, now sly and prankish way of consort-
ing with politicians in the East and the West—all
this popularity did not make his verses popular. A
second edition of *Die Vorzüge der Windhühner* came
out only in 1963, still at the ridiculously low price
of $1.20. His second volume of lyrics, too—entitled
Gleisdreieck [Railroad-track Triangle] (1960), with
eighteen illustrations by the author, some of them
double-paged—had few buyers.

This latter collection of fifty poems contains
some themes that had already appeared in the first
collection. It made still more evident how one-sided
it had been earlier (using the harsh dissonances and
a few autobiographical elements of *The Tin Drum*
as points of reference) to see in Günter Grass only a
frenzied amoralist running berserk. Grass is a tem-
peramental, passionate man, but at the same time a
very careful and deliberate artist. A profound artistic sense prevents him from "beating the drum at
random." Metaphorically speaking, at times he
seems to me like a thrifty, even parsimonious head
of the family, unwilling to part from metaphors and
themes, objects and ideas which have become dear
to him. He conceals, buries, forgets, or would like
to forget them. And then they re-emerge—altered, de-
formed, inflated, or gnawed away to grotesquely
warped skeletons—into the light of dawn or the high
noon of a new day, masked by a naïveté that kills,
since evil things have their value and place everywhere, even in the process of the creation of art.
Eight lines of verse—titled "Der Dichter" [The Poet]
—their ending almost sentimental, gently evoke his

grief and mourning for warm and helpless life that
has been destroyed:

> Evil,
> As only a Sütterlin script can be evil,
> He spreads out on lined paper.
> All the children can read him,
> And they run away
> And tell it to the rabbits,
> And the rabbits die, become extinct—
> Ink for whom, when rabbits are no more?

Oskar Matzerath, the obstinate tin drummer of
an infantile age, sees on the photo of his first school
day the initial letter M in Sütterlin script. From the
hidden memory of a document covered with Sütterlin script, containing photos of the destruction of the
Warsaw ghetto, the school-days idyl receives the
horribly grotesque tincture of ineradicable evil,
which is immortal for the very reason that it has the
ability to mask itself as serenity and harmony again
and again.

For the most part Günter Grass's imagination
takes fire in poetry and in epic and dramatic prose
focused on things. Things dominate mankind, determine situations, force the age under their spell.
Things unleash demonism, and they bind and sub-
due it. In the lyric volume *Gleisdreieck*, Diana, god-
dess of the night, is appealed to as the patroness of
poets, in a poem entitled, "Diana—oder die Gegenstände" [Diana, or the Objects]:

> When with her right hand she reaches
> Over her right shoulder into the quiver,
> She puts her left leg forward.

When she hit me,
Her object hit my soul,
Which is to her like an object. . . .

When she says yes and hits,
She hits the objects in nature
But also stuffed ones.

I always refused
To let my shadow-casting body
Be hurt by a shadowless idea.

But you, Diana,
With your bow
Are to me like an object, and liable.

The outline of a new mythology, as it becomes visible in the work of Günter Grass, includes the object-based dialectic of the young Karl Marx, but enlarges it by means of references that have been, if not excluded, at least badly neglected by the writers who represent the world in more or less "socialist", more or less "realist" terms. Diana's arrow strikes objects, including objects in nature, not just stuffed objects, but also the soul, "which is to her like an object."

Out of the counterreaction to the object, movement results, the life process, a dialectic by which limits are fixed and limits abolished. The process has been known for ages and is not at all mechanically or materially fixed, at least in the sense that some formula or law can predict its course in advance with surety. The poet, today as in the time of Homer able to penetrate uncharted regions, takes us by the hand. He gives contour to the expiring dream. He enlarges, with the help of new varieties of humor—

Christian Morgenstern comes to mind—the dialectic of objects; he establishes new cross references between otherwise unconnected invisible objects (by isolating them). After the fashion of Wilhelm Busch and Morgenstern, Ringelnatz and Hans Arp, nonsense poetry continues in Günter Grass. With their originality of approach the scherzo "Der elfte Finger" and "Die Schule der Tenöre" prove that Grass is one of the above company. So do some of the four-, five-, and six-line poems in the first lyric volume. The simplest—positively exemplary—proof is the little étude "Tierschutz" [Prevention of Cruelty to Animals]:

> The piano goes into the zoo.
> Quick, get the zebra into the best room.
> Be nice to it,
> It comes out of Bechstein.
> It feeds on music notes
> And our sweet ears.

The cunning of the object—which since Friedrich Theodor Vischer's *Auch Einer* [Another One] has become an idea for us, a formula, almost a philistine cliché—became virulent in a manner unsuspected, when Günter Grass began with unfettered, fascinating bravura and virtuosity to describe the cunning of a child's toy, a tin drum. There is a measured, classical sound to a remark that Goethe makes in the *Italian Journey:* "Every object, rightly regarded, unlocks a new organ in us." But what happens when children's eyes regard a drum? When the senses of a newborn child are awakened by a moth's wings beating against an electric light bulb?

Is the object in this case "rightly" or "not rightly" regarded—who is to decide? And just to regard the object in a certain perspective—with a sidelong glance, or through eyes filled with tears—does not this alone awaken in us something unexpected, mysterious, and terrifying?

An object in nature, the father, alters the objects as the children see them. The altered objects alter the gaze of the children. The children's altered gaze alter an object in nature that was not altered to begin with: the father. This is an example, another example, of the dialectic of objects, which is set forth with mathematical and poetic precision in the poem "Der Vater" [The Father].

The dramaturgy of the scene which determines this poem, as well as almost all other poems of Günter Grass, determines in a similar way the proceedings in his plays, stories, and novels. In fact, when one thinks of the point of departure or the climax, or any moment in the successive phases of the proceedings, one could also include his sketches, charcoal drawings, and watercolors. The moment, with its arrangement of the things, decides the conception of the scene. It is drafted, now on the sketch pad as a drawing, now as lines of verse, or in epic or dramatic form. Sometimes the possibilities in this or that genre are played through successively or simultaneously. It is then seen that—despite all the signs that laws governing respective literary forms are being relaxed or are disintegrating, despite all the effacing of boundaries between different genres—unrescindable generic laws continue to hold good.

In a few cases—perhaps not meant to be taken quite seriously—Grass has given reasons for preferring one genre or another. Expediency may play a part, rational explanations too may now and again be of significance—but neither these arguments nor purely technical criteria have decisive weight. The question of whether something has come off successfully or not, the quality of the work of art in its entirety and in its integral parts—a stanza, a dramatic or epic scene—is dependent primarily on the tension arising out of the dialectic of objects and on the resolution of that tension. In Grass there are unexpected combinations, frequently on successive lines, chain reactions of scintillating and weirdly farcical ideas, which often unfold in grandiose cadenzas and at the close are curbed in an austere coda. But there are also effects that miscarry, points that are not sharp, tedium and banality, mechanism for mechanism's sake.

If one measures the value of artistic work by its success, if one judges a book by its sales and by the amount of public sensation it creates, the primary position, in Grass's case, must be occupied by *The Tin Drum*. Most reviewers in fact recognize only Grass the novelist and story writer. His lyric and dramatic works, his manifold activities in the realm of the fine arts, are for them marginal. It is of course undeniable that, with regard to their range, their thematic significance, the variety of their style elements, and their well-rounded and richly differentiated main themes, the novels *The Tin Drum* and *Dog Years* deserve special attention. Nevertheless it

would be a mistake to consider these his solely decisive works, works besides which Grass's other pro-
ductions carry hardly any weight. In actuality the
three literary forms (poetry, plays, and novels) are
of equal rank for him, at least in the drafting stage.
Sometimes Grass plays out the theme in all three
forms concurrently, alternates the tone, improvises.
I can imagine that, when he played the washboard
in a jazz band during his days as an art student in
Düsseldorf about 1950, he took many a hint for the
writing of poems, plays, and chapters of novels from
jazz. A studied monotony, exactly calculated dis-
placements, and *pizzicati* passages are as characteristic of his work as is the disappearance and re-
emergence of melody.

3

My Room
Is Sheltered
from the Wind

Transitions from poem to poem, from a line of verse to a dialogue in a play, a story, a novel. Behind the brittle and the fragmentary, which, conditioned by the times and by art, often stand side by side unconnected, recalling now Dadaism and the montage art of the 1920's, now surrealism and pop art, there sways and rumbles, bubbles and throbs, sparkles and vibrates, in Günter Grass a vitality that seems to have its origin in pagan times. The process through which mankind has passed since antiquity, since the Renaissance, can be interpreted psychologically or sociologically—with Karl Marx—as a process of self-alienation. One can also—starting with Hegel and proceeding via Lukacs and Walter Benjamin to Adorno—seek to understand the same process in poetry as a dialectic of content and form. Whatever the approach, the situation of man can be given shape only if within this dialectic, the dialectic of person and objects, the poet possesses sufficient freedom and elementary inventiveness to be simultaneously in action within this process and outside it.

Because Günter Grass has strong imaginative and inventive power, he has freedom to carry the process of our becoming to consummation in a poem, to draw the inner and the future course into its meaning, and at the end to throw the whole thing into doubt by means of a humor that ridicules not what is uncanny but only the presumption that would exclude it. This he does while relativizing himself and his artistic creation—in reality, ourselves. The following poem is titled "Im Ei" [In the Egg]:

We live in the egg.
Over the inside wall of the shell
We have scribbled dirty drawings
And our enemies' first names.
We are being hatched. . . .

And what if we are not being hatched?
If this shell never breaks open?
If our horizon is only the horizon
Of our scribbles, and will stay that way?
We hope that we are being hatched.

Even if we only talk about hatching,
There is still the fear that someone
Outside our shell will feel hungry
And break us into the frying pan with a sprinkle of salt.
What shall we do then, brothers in the egg?

One could call this didactic poem a mixture of Morgenstern and Ringelnatz, a parody of Schiller's idealistic world concept, of the cultivation of an "inner realm" (including the "inner emigration"), perhaps even a parody of a pessimistic ethic's deviant form, existentialism of the Sartre type. One could even say that in this poem the man who proclaimed the "will to power" is invited into the kitchen of sound human intellect, where he is shown what it looks like in practice when one philosophizes with a hammer. All this and more could be noted. But perhaps it may be more enlightening or amusing to take this poem, and much else that Grass has produced, as a game, a joke. In turn we must not take this "playful joking" interpretation so deadly seriously that we make an absolute of it, echoing for the thousandth time Schiller's dictum that "man is entirely man only when he is at play." Only man? Not

the cat also? Not Satan, the Mephistopheles of
Goethe, Grabbe, et al.? The role that the mice and
rats play can be read in Grass. He has crazier things
to tell us than Brehm, a few chapters of whom he
has studied very closely.

In the two-act play *The Flood*, for example,
after the cloudburst is over and a beautiful rainbow
is on the horizon, the rats Perle and Strich look at
the glorious spectrum of colors. Strich broods:
"What these colors make me think of—I could become a convert to anthroposophism on the spot."
"I'd much rather nibble," says the practical-minded
Perle.

Let us not press more useless nibbling on the
symbol-mocking, already overworked rodents of
Günter Grass. Let us think of the fact that in the
lyric volume *Gleisdreieck,* in addition to the poem
about Racine and the rats, there are forty-nine other
poems, some of them very good. Let us remember
too that rats are part of this world. Rats and voles in
the dikes of the Vistula lowland in *Dog Years*. They
infiltrate the protecting wall; they infiltrate the book
and its interpretation. Let us avoid them. Let us, in
closing this chapter, stick to Grass the lyricist. If he
wants to make his poems firmly and unassailably a
"creation to be handed on to posterity" (Benn), he
must sit at the wind-sheltered, motionless center of
this uniformly and agitatedly rotating world and
"place a mystic spell on things by the power of the
word" (Benn). This central point is the property of
the lyric. Either one reaches this center or he does
not. One cannot find it or lose it at will, paint it or

not paint it (as some contemporaries continue to think, freely or nonfreely applying Hans Sedl-mayer). One cannot gain it by counting syllables any more than by contemplating devout paintings, even though it can scarcely be denied that children and mystics—even mystics without a God—have the easiest access to it. Is Günter Grass a mystic without a God? He is regarded as a rabid fellow. Strictly believing Catholics are not the only ones who accuse him of blasphemy. Other, more mod-erate Catholic reviewers point to the fact that the drum-beating, glass-shattering dwarf Oskar has no power over church windows—a fine stroke, very significant, say these critics. I do not know—perhaps this is just a joke intended to mislead, a trap for interpretation addicts. At any rate, the following appeared in the *Spiegel* of September 4, 1963:

Blasphemy and anticlericalism in Grass's work have a pecu-liar correspondence with the Catholic origins of the Danzig author, who sees "no reason to leave the Church" and has his children raised as Catholics: they can "Later on see for themselves what goes on there."

(Will these children, when they have become adults and perhaps strict Catholics, also notice what "is going on" with their father?)

The question of whether Günter Grass is a mystic without a God, or indeed a mystic at all, might be answered in the affirmative or the negative. The undeniable fact remains that as a lyric poet he has written a "Credo," and that to this "Credo" and many another of his poems, and to some passages in his plays and novels too, the following dictum of

Georg Lukacs—*Die Theorie des Romans* [The Theory of the Novel] (page 49)—applies: "Every creative subjectivity becomes lyrical. Only the subjectivity that simply accepts, that meekly transforms itself into a sheer receptive organ of the world is able to share in grace, that is, in the revelation of the whole."

The young Lukacs speaks of meekness and grace, and of the revelation of the whole. That does not sound Marxist; rather it sounds conservative, faced understandingly toward the picture of St. Jerome. And since, as Dostoevsky says, history is the doctrine that deals with the future, the grace we have just alluded to also holds true now for Grass, the cigarette-smoking hermit who has read the Bible and that evangelist of surrealism Breton as well as Eluard, Arp, and Morgenstern, *Alice in Wonderland*, and children's rhymes in many languages. He sits in the sheltered center of the typhoon and thinks of the last days of the war, when he was wounded at Cottbus. He saw the shipwreck, saw the shipwreck of those who were saved, and said—against all reason, all probability—"We shall never run aground." He says this in his "Credo":

> My room is sheltered from the wind,
> Pious, a cigarette,
> So mystic that no one dares
> To collect rent
> Or asks about my wife.
> Yesterday when the fly died,
> I understood without a calendar,
> It's October, a dancing teacher bows,
> Wants to sell me little forbidden pictures.
> I receive callers outside my door,

> The mail sticks to the pane
> Outside, the rain reads it too.
> Inside, my room is sheltered,   S 1523438
> No strife on wallpaper,
> Kisses swallowed by clocks,
> Never stumble, bump my knee,
> Because everything gives way,
> Pious, a cigarette,
> Perpendicular is its belief,
> Perpendicularly the spider takes a sounding,
> Investigates every shoal,
> We shall never run aground.

I do not know in what sheltered studio in Düsseldorf, Berlin, or elsewhere, Günter Grass wrote these lines. He has been married since 1954 to a Swiss dancer, Anna Margaretha Schwarz. They moved into a bomb-damaged house in the Grunewald district of Berlin—they had four rooms at 16 Karlsbader Straße. There, with their three children (Franz and Raoul—the twins—and Laura, who is three years younger), they lived till the end of 1963, when they moved to Friedenau.

With Berlin, the city that has been occupied by foreign military powers since 1945, a new, dark motif has come into the literary and artistic work of Günter Grass. This is attested to by three of the strongest poems in the lyric volume *Gleisdreieck*. The spider from the framed picture of St. Jerome has changed. Three times on the dust jacket, on the cover, and again (somewhat modified) in the interior of the volume it gapes out at us. Its body has black hatching and it crouches weirdly, stilted legs and body curved in a steely arc, at a deadly dangerous rail junction of the city. What the charcoal drawing only half discloses is stated openly, revealing want and the treachery of want, in the title poem:

> Railroad-track triangle, where with hot gland
> The spider that lays the tracks
> Made its home and lays the tracks.
>
> It merges seamlessly into bridges
> And drives rivets itself afterward
> If rivets are loosened by what comes into the net.

When Grass wrote this poem, the charwomen were still making their daily trips from the East Sector of the city to the West undisturbed. Since August 13, 1961, that has changed. Grass's poem tells history. But the threatening thing has already been told in this story:

> We travel often and show our friends,
> Here is railroad-track triangle, get out here
> And count tracks with your fingers.
>
> The switches beckon, charwomen travel,
> The taillight means me, but the spider
> Catches flies and lets charwomen travel.
> We stare credulously into the gland
> And read what the gland writes:
> Railroad-track triangle, you are leaving at once
>
> Railroad-track triangle and the West Sector.

Not since Georg Heym in the lyric form and Alfred Döblin in the epic *(Alexanderplatz, Berlin)* has the city on the Spree been portrayed with such power and precision, in images that correspond to this fateful hour, as in the three poems "Die große

Trümmerfrau" [The Big Rubble Woman Speaks],
"Gleisdreieck" [Railroad-track Triangle], and
"Brandmauern" [Fireproof Walls]. Here is "Brand-
mauern":

> I greet Berlin, three times
> Beating my forehead three times
> On one of the fireproof walls.

A hard cantata of words is heard in the poem
about the big rubble woman, who considers Wilhel-
minian mortar nothing and spits into the "pregnant
cement-mixing machine." The echo and shadow of
the rubble woman lurk amid the remnants of the
wall. The children sing about the bet that the brick-
maker has made with them; the object is lots of
rubble. The lament ends thus:

> Amen, amen.
> Berlin lies strewn about.
> Dust flies up,
> Then stagnation again.
> The big rubble woman is canonized.

Besides the three significant Berlin poems, the
second volume of lyrics contains a few poems scenic
in structure and arranged in several movements.
These poems are interesting, for one thing, because
—now in the form of a suite, now as a rondo, now
as a folksong with modified refrain—they anticipate
or replay themes in the great novels. Thus "Laments
bei Regen" [Lament on a Rainy Day] quotes the
"tin drum verse":

> You shouldn't get so upset,
> It's not raining because of you.

The motif of the eel roaming over the meadows appears, along with the first jokes about scarecrows, still undemonic, gay, though with an undercurrent of meaning already present:

> I don't know what incubates in hats,
> What slips out from what thoughts
> And begins to fly and does not let itself be scared away;
> We are guarded by scarecrows.

Strictly constructed and casually joined stanzas, the wondrous metamorphosis of the doll Nana, ending in the afternoon:

> The doll fell into the tea,
> Dissolved like sugar in the tea—
> And those who drank it emerged from their cocoons
> Until one doll looked like another.

Twelve-tone music of objects; verses from children's games; disagreement with a particular phrase—"Meine Hühner lachen nicht" [My Chickens Aren't Laughing]; the tinny educational game in the dialectic of "Köche und Löffel" [Cooks and Spoons]; a farcical scene from the absurd monodrama—"Frost und Gebiß" [Frost and False Teeth]; marital strife recited through its declension of successive destroyed or damaged objects—"Inventar oder die Ballade von der zerbrochenen Vase" [Inventory, or The Ballad of the Broken Vase]; nuns who continue to stir the extravagant fancy of the nature boy from the Vistula lowlands. With wide-open eyes he looks after them, lets himself be carried back to the time of Elizabeth by their wide black veils, and practices "magic with the brides of Christ."

There is much else, such as the dark poem "Saturn," which could be in a school reader (for upper classes). Also "Pan Kiehot," the Polish Don Quixote who at Kutno rode into the hard flank of German armor, belongs in a school reader (for middle classes). And likewise, of course, "Kinderlied" [Children's Song]:

> Who is laughing here, who has laughed?
> Here the laughing is over and done with.

The quintessence of an age is in what I felt to be the most powerfully moving, shocking poem in this collection. It is named "Adebar" [The Stork].

> Time was here when grain was heavy on the stem,
> And storks stood on the chimneys;
> From its body the fifth child slips away.

> For a long time I did not know there were yet storks,
> That to storks a chimney without smoke
> Is the same as a finger pointed.

> Dead is the factory, but overhead adolescent storks
> Are the smoke that, white, red-legged,
> Settles on damp meadows.

> Time was when in Treblinka on Sundays
> There was much smoking flesh, stork-blessed,
> Heated air by which the gliders cleared the ground.

> That was in Poland, where the Virgin Mary
> Stiffly rides on storks,
> But—when the stem falls—flees into Egypt.

By the year 1966, Günter Grass the lyric poet had still not been discovered. In both collections of his poetry there are weak poems, to be sure. When a world of fairy tale, a world of myth, has been

broken into pieces, how can a children's rhyme save
it? Georg Büchner told the story of how in the
mouth of the grandmother the colorful burgeoning
world becomes dust and ashes, how the sun becomes
an overturned jar, a chamber pot on which a child
sits weeping. Grass bends over the weeping child.
He beats his forehead against the fireproof wall. He
hears the lament of the rubble woman. He does not
harmonize the dissonances of the time. Sometimes
he misses. Sometimes he succeeds in capturing, in an
image or a movement of images, what eludes the
grasp of other authors. The elemental naive com-
ponent of his nature is combined with a feigned
naiveté, a virtuoso's love of game playing that not
infrequently exceeds the boundary respected by less
aggressive authors as the limit of propriety. Liberal
critics object, too, that in his novels Grass, though
he is often great at describing things that are shocking, enjoys his own virtuosity in doing so all too
much. This reproach was leveled against the young
Schiller in his own time, against the young Gerhart
Hauptmann, and the Brecht who wrote *Baal*, and,
in our day, not infrequently against Sartre, Beckett,
Genet, and others.

A greater danger than the foaming exuberance
—even if the foam is occasionally dirty—seems to
me to lie in the fact that Günter Grass (his friend
Walter Höllerer once reproached him with this)
often relies too much on the tangibly dependable
that "has the ready phrase in stock and produces it."
Thus there are "vacant passages" in his lyrics, his
novels, and especially his plays. And there are

objects, such as favorite animals, that the reader cannot possibly have as high a regard for as the author does. Since the monotony is a studied monotony, since it is employed as a device of art just as surely as in monochromatic painting, there remains the question of when and to what extent it achieves effects that are artistically pure or, on the other hand, not entirely satisfying. The play, with its broader unfolding of themes, offers a better ground than the lyric poem for expounding this question.

4

Many Cooks
and No Recipe

In a group discussion on October 19, 1961, in Hamburg, Günter Grass had this to say regarding the road that led him to the drama:

Till now I have written lyrics, plays, and prose. For me all three disciplines, even the lyric, are built upon dialogue. So the way that the transition from lyric to theater play was accomplished was that poems were written in dialogue form, and expanded. Then slowly and by degrees stage directions were added, and in this way—on the side, besides my then chief calling, sculpture—I evolved my first play. I therefore wrote in a relatively short time, from 1954 to 1957, four plays and two one-act pieces, which, just like my lyrics and my prose, have in them fantastic and realistic elements that exert friction and control on each other. . . .

During the conversation, in which young German authors discussed with play editors and critics the theme "Schreiben fürs Theater: Vergnügen oder Verdruß?" [Writing for the Theater: Enjoyment or Vexation?], Grass sat rather discontentedly between colleagues who, then at any rate, had greater successes to show in the field of theater. Tancred Dorst had written *Große Schmährede an der Stadtmauer* [Great Diatribe at the City Wall]; Dieter Waldmann, *Von Bergamo bis morgen früh* [From Bergamo to Tomorrow Morning]; and Siegfried Lenz, *Zeit der Schuldlosen* [The Time of the Guiltless]. With an expression that was cheerful and in a voice that sounded a little vexed, Grass said that the people in Germany whose job it is to adapt plays for stage production were to blame for his having thus far had less success as a stage writer than in the field of the prose epic:

Prose has a well-functioning market thanks to the book trade. For plays there has so far been an impediment: the play adapter. For me the crisis of the theater was less in the playwriting itself, for there are the same difficulties—of course, in a different area—in writing a play as in writing a poem or a novel. But the real problem was my relations with the play adapters.

This revealed a quality in Grass that had struck me at our first meeting and several times afterwards: the immediately dramatic element in his character. Sometimes I think, "How well he stages his entries and exits." Then I tell myself that that is his nature. But this nature has an effect like witchcraft. Suddenly he is standing in a group of people who did not expect him. Just as suddenly he had disappeared. In the labyrinthine corridors of the West Berlin Academy of Arts, I have always had the impression that Grass does not come through doorways; he steps into the house directly through the wall. He invents excuses, even persons, when he wishes to stay away from a reception: "My twin brother is visiting me." "Bring him with you this evening." "Ah, no, then we'd use each other up too fast."

In the Hamburg discussion, his account of his relations with play adapters had the same dramatic quality:

First I tried being shy with them, because I had never seen any before. Then I was advised to be friendly with them. That was no help either. Then I became resigned. So you see in me a stage writer who is resigned to his lot. I traveled the opposite road to that of Herr Lenz; I went from theater to prose, and that was—naturally it was, when you go from theater to prose—dramatic; I had to take an oath. Following a performance in Cologne I took the oath: "Now you are going to write no more plays until all the plays you have written have been performed and are back for a second run." That means I have time yet, and so I am occupying myself with prose for a while, and have made a virtue of necessity. In short, I am writing dramatic prose and later perhaps it will work the other way round and we shall again have an epic theater.

The dramaturgists (play adapters) assembled in Hamburg politely refrained from asking whether the main fault for the small interest on the part of directors in second runs of Grass's plays really lay with people of the theater or rather in deficiencies in the plays themselves. Meanwhile Marianne Kesting, in her paperback volume *Panorama des zeitgenössischen Theaters* [Panorama of the Contemporary Theater] (1962), has judged Grass very severely. "It is significant for the exponents of the German theater of the absurd, among whom Grass must be numbered, that sociological pertinence is just the quality in which they are lacking. They avail themselves of the means employed by the French absurdists, not for social analysis, but to play a more or less amusing game; they operate with flashing scenic ideas, with startling imagistic stage effects which do not signify much and are evidently not intended to. The whole world seems absurd to them, and they leave the public in the dark as to which world is absurd and why."

Two years after this criticism went to press, Günter Grass broke his Cologne oath and exercised self-criticism. At any rate, this conclusion is suggested by the fact that he has withdrawn one of his still unperformed plays—*Zweiunddreißig Zähne* [Thirty-

two Teeth] and has set himself to writing works
for the stage again. In so doing he did not cover
his retreat very skillfully, but chose to offer a
play "cribbed" from one of his novels. He took a
chapter from *Dog Years* that was written in dialogue form, and, in June, 1964, had it performed
in the workshop theater of the Munich Kammer-
spiele under the title *Goldmäulchen.* The whole
thing, according to Erich Pfeiffer-Belli, "amounted
at most to a somewhat long-winded joke and not a
bitter indictment." Critics such as Wolfgang Drews
and Joachim Kaiser, whose reviews of the performance were as detailed as they were unfavorable,
found that this offering of what the author had
called "dramatic" prose did not, or at any rate not
yet, mark the transition to the "epic theater" of
which he had spoken in the discusssion in Hamburg.

But let us return to Grass's first plays and
follow his directions in presenting and interpreting
those six dramatic works that were created in a
relatively short time. The first one-act play, *Beritten
hin und zurück* [Mounted Going There and
Coming Back] (1954), was followed in 1955 by
the two-act play *The Flood* (revised in 1962). In
1956, *Mister, Mister,* a play in four acts, was completed. The year 1957 saw completion of, besides
the one-act play *Only Ten Minutes to Buffalo,* the
five-act drama *The Wicked Cooks,* and 1958 (in a
version that its author no longer validates) the grotesque piece *Zweiunddreißig Zähne.*

The Brecht pupil and opera director Egon
Monk, who is the head of television production in
Hamburg, laughingly related to me the content of

this play, which is probably just a joke, a farce that
pokes fun at the hygiene campaign that continues to
spread in our time. The hero of this grotesque piece
is persecuted by a teacher named Purucker, a fana-
tic about taking care of the teeth who appears everywhere brandishing a toothbrush. He turns up in the
privacy of the bathroom. He appears again in the
midst of the vast mountains of Switzerland that once
bore witness to the Rütli Oath of William Tell. The
quarry attempts to flee across the ocean, and the
pursuer enters his cabin through the porthole. More
strongly than in the case of other plays, plays that I
have read or seen performed on the stage, the individual scenes of this piece which was subsequently
narrated to me are still visually clear in my memory.
Basically it is always the same situation, repeated in
fantastic variation and in grotesque intensification.
Pouring out its theatrical store with precision
timing, surprising one with its turns of plot and
gags, it makes an imprint on the memory like a
clown's act in a circus. Here, it seems to me—
leaving aside any evaluation of the details of its
artistic execution—we have a play by Grass that is
gifted and has originality. In addition there is his
tendency, already stressed in his lyrics, to use the
object as a point of departure and to represent it,
not man, as the active and activating element.

   This dialectic of objects—sometimes it is a
simple inversion, even an inversion of currently
fashionable ideas, phrases, modes of behavior, and
clichés of social action—are the sustenance of
poems and epic and dramatic scenes in the work of

Günter Grass. Sometimes they are penetrating and rich in flashes of wit, sometimes silly and banal, as in the four-act play *Mister, Mister*. This play is about the murderer Bollin, a frustrated lover of order and system. In the prelude the murderer is sitting slumped on a park bench while a thirteen-year-old girl, Sprotte, and a fourteen-year-old boy, Janne-mann, talk about him in the way that understanding adults talk about poor social misfits: "He probably hasn't got a father or mother any more." "And at home he was the only child, too." They ask him: "Mister, mister? Are ya lonesome? Ain't ya got somethin' for us mister?" Mister has—candy. "Cheap stuff," say the children and talk like adults about candy's injurious effect on the teeth. They sing their song, which they sing again at the close of the play (after they have taken the murderer's revolver from him and shot him with it):

> Mister, mister, ain't ya got a thing,
> Mister, just a little thing,
> Any little thing.

The "thing" (revolver) is "lifted," and when it is the police endeavor to arrest the evildoer. In the object there is a power that acts according to its own laws. When it detaches itself from man and becomes autonomous, it retains a remarkable demonism, an ambivalence, the effect of which is that the "nature of things" turns now to the good, now to the bad. Parallel to the process that the sociologists term self-alienation, there runs through modern drama a development in which objects increasingly obtain more independence and greater specific gravity. In Heinrich von Kleist the object is a broken jug; in Gerhart Hauptmann, a beaver fur; in Zuckmayer, the military uniform of the shoemaker Voigt; in Dürrenmatt, the coffin of the old lady Zachanassian; in Ionesco's *Amédé, or How Does One Get Rid of Him?*, it is a corpse which jerkily pushes itself into an old couple's living room. ("Nothing can be done about it," says the husband. "It's got geometrical progression, the incurable disease of the dead.")

In the four preludes and four acts of *Mister, Mister*, the autonomy and ambivalence of objects appears in a more harmless form, sometimes in the manner of the comic weeklies, sometimes colored by the spectacles of a black humor. It is objects that prevent the murderer Bollin from carrying out his plans for murder. Objects that distract him, such as Pinkie, the doll of the teenager Sophie, who is in bed with the grippe. Or an object that people do not take seriously: his revolver. Sophie's mother says, "You left your whatsis lying there, on the night table. Do you always have it on you?" "Sometimes," says Bollin. Frau Domke is friendly. "Gosh, why not?" she agrees. "My husband always used to carry a little tin automobile in his pocket. We all have our ways." Grass has fun presenting man's childlike reactions and his manipulation of things, and presenting them in many variations, harmlessly and uncannily, mischievously and murderously. In the prelude to Act Two, entitled "Der Kuckuck" [The Cuckoo], he has the murderer Bollin use the doll Pinkie for stabbing and shooting practice. The gamekeeper Forschbach, whom Bollin is about to bury alive in a pit (as he did the gamekeeper Platzmann and two apprentices) is saved by objects of nature, a couple of pine cones that the teenagers Sprotte and Jannemann throw into the pit. Since it is dark in the pit, he is to "c'mup f'r a minute" to "explain" them to the children. The murderer agrees, and the game-keeper explains about the conifers and the sand in which they grow. He enlarges on the subject of the scrub pine, which is also known as dwarf pine. The children are fascinated by the word: "Why dwarf?" "Well," the gamekeeper explains, "in those regions there are entirely different weather conditions, and a slender tree can't live there. That is why the scrub pine . . . stays small and seems to us like a bush, and crippled. Now let's say it once more. That is why the . . ." And while the children recite halt-ingly, and the gamekeeper prompts and the children repeat, the gamekeeper unnoticed walks away, and Bollin shovels the soil back into the empty pit. It is a musical, almost liturgical, end to the second act.

Bollin is by no means always frustrated as a murderer, and shifts from gamekeepers to barbers, from barbers to stage celebrities. Now he seeks his victim among female opera singers, and the third act shows how he fails with the soprano Mimi Landella —and she with him. The diva, who is engaged to a photographer—whom she calls "You flashbulb!"— does anything for publicity. For publicity she arranges to have herself murdered, because she sees in the possibility of being murdered by Bollin the chance of a lifetime. But in her eagerness to have the murder scene photographed in just the right colors, she overdoes it. The murderer, without having achieved his purpose, says, "I've had enough, I'm through with the opera," and walks out.

In the fourth act, which is a consistent extension of the prelude to Act One, the children Jannemann and Sprotte "dispatch" the murderer. So ends the problem that in the first three acts was played around with in a more or less witty and jocular way but which, in terms of dialectic and drama, was not explored thoroughly or effectively. The all-dominating, all-threatening object, the revolver, the "thing," is filched from the murderer by the children in a game played with childish cunning, is used as a toy, and—by the very fact that it murders the murderer—becomes "free" in its full dangerous ambivalence and autonomy as an object. Thus in the closing act the limits of the theme—stated in the latent tension of the opening situation and revealed and set free in its sinister character at the end—are demonstrated. Not only can it be seen that the absence of the sociological pertinence which Marianne Kesting noted in Grass is in theme and basic situation—in the irresponsible handling of murderous objects—but also that the dramaturgic execution lacks that severity, precision, and force of attack which an author like Dürrenmatt, who also employs the grotesque, for the most part possesses in high degree.

In the discussion sponsored by the Dramaturgic Society in Hamburg, Grass had said that his plays, "just like [my] lyrics and prose, have in them fantastic and realistic elements that exert friction and control on each other." In this conversation he had at first censured the dramaturgists' inaction, their deficient zeal for replaying his stage works. Somewhat later, however, he complained of their false and contradictory activity. On the one hand (he said) they demanded good stagecraft, on the other hand they maintained that clearly delineated conclusions of acts were no longer possible in the experimental theater and "theater of the absurd" of our day. "After a few years," he continued, "one gets tired of arguing with them [over the fact] that, if foreign authors are cited, there is after all a difference between Adamov and Ionesco and that both are descended from Büchner and Kleist. Why," he asked in conclusion, "shouldn't German authors derive directly and without detour from Büchner and Kleist?"

There is little to be found of Büchner and Kleist in *Mister, Mister*. But in the poetically richer plays, such as *The Flood, The Wicked Cooks*, and *Only Ten Minutes to Buffalo*, (the one-act favorite of student dramatic groups), there are romantic and fantastic-realistic elements that are definitely reminiscent of Kleist and the marionette-like movements of the figures in Büchner's *Leonce und Lena*. Of course these (incidentally very sparse) elements and motifs are not merely taken over and mechanistically assembled; they not only exert friction on each other in their fantastic and realistic aspects, but they also control each other, at least in the successful scenes.

Rather than attempt a more or less comprehensive and exact definition of the theater of the
absurd and to fix the place of Günter Grass on the
basis of such a definition, it seems to me more fruit-
ful to make an interpretation that takes for its
starting point the prerequisites that the author
regards as intrinsic for himself. Best suited for such
an investigation is the "object"—often mentioned in
this book before—or, to be more exact, the content.
In other words, precisely that which critics and historians of literature—each according to his antece-
dents and the aesthetics he was once taught—praise
or damn, term important or trivial, and place in
more or less exact relation to the form. Very popular in this procedure are antithetical couplings
such as *avant-garde* and *traditional, progressive* and
reactionary, etc. Grass does not exclude this coup-
ling of antithetical concepts. But he takes them less
seriously than do the professors of aesthetics. He
plays with them, plays with sovereign authority,
and, full of enjoyment, he discovers in this game
new stimuli, new combinations, new nuances. For
naturally he knows very well—what many of his
critics do not know—that the game with objects
before Kandinsky (and the discovery of abstract or
objectless art) is different from that game *since*
Kandinsky. One now plays with what was once dead
earnest, plays with concepts, with the antithetical
pairs *content* and *form, reaction* and *progress, avant-
gardism* and *tradition*. This playing with art concepts itself becomes a part of art. The *objectless* is
included in the dialectical game and becomes itself

an object; it negates the negative in which the abstract threatens to dissolve. The poem "Diana —oder die Gegenstände," as we have seen, captures the process in an image.

No less suitable for capturing the process in an image or a series of images is the epic or dramatic account. Another way is the wordless transition from drawing and sculpture into movement, for example in ballet. The ballet libretto is sometimes a kind of preparatory form or advance exercise for the drama. In Grass's first ballet, *Fünf Köche* [Five Cooks] which was first performed in France under Marcel Luitpart, can be recognized some favorite figures of Grass the artist as well as Grass the dramatist and storyteller. Because a second ballet, entitled *Stoffreste* [Material Remnants], was performed in Essen and, despite good reviews, was "buried" and not given a second run, Grass lost the desire to write any more ballets. In the novel *Dog Years* we may read what can become of such a theme when developed as an epic. (In the discussion with the dramaturgists in Hamburg, Grass had said, "The creation of a ballet libretto can be wonderfully recast in prose, and then one does not have the annoyance afterward with the theater.")

In the volume *Theater—Wahrheit und Wirklichkeit* [Theater: Truth and Reality] (Zurich, 1962), which was presented to Kurt Hirschfeld on his sixtieth birthday, Peter Löffler makes an important comment on "Zum Thema Gegenstand und Mensch im Modernen Drama" [The Theme of the Object and Man in Modern Drama]. Löffler points to the reduction of the individual in the stage works of the present day. In contrast to this downward valuation of man, there is (he writes) an upward valuation of objects. Modern drama is inclined "to invest objects with at least a potential power that at times can become a magical one."

The magical object, Löffler says, is to be regarded as "a kind of secularized relic," like the furniture of the "new tenant" and the chairs in Eugène Ionesco's play *The New Tenant*. This alteration that is taking place with regard to the object and man in modern drama might be characterized as "a tendency to transform the human into the inorganic and a tendency to transform the objective into the organic." In the realm of metaphor, Löffler continues, there are, as we know, comparisons whereby something living is represented by means of something without life, and something lifeless by means of something living. In the objectification of living beings and the animating of dead things, it is as if these metaphoric forms were running rampant. The metaphor is not only used in words but is extended to the total represented reality."

The last remark is of particular importance for judging the optics which determine the entire ouput of Günter Grass: pictorial work and stagecraft, lyric and epic writing, even "occasional" pieces dealing with topics of the day, short essays on the clown, the ballerina, and questions of aesthetics and poetry. They are all part of the cosmos of a world of images in which realistic and grotesque elements encounter each other in new combinations as well as in tried and proved ones. In the essay, as in other forms, these elements exert friction and control on each other. Of great importance is the article by Grass that appeared in the bimonthly *Akzente* in June, 1957, under the title, "Der Inhalt als Widerstand" [The Content as Resistance].

This treatise, which can be regarded as the nucleus of his aesthetics, is followed by a "mistrustful dialogue" between the poets Pempelfort and Krudewil. (Two figures with these names, disguised as train engineer and fireman, appear in the one-act play *Only Ten Minutes to Buffalo*.) Following the romantic model, the dialogue of ideas changes into a disputation between Pempelfort, the "poet linked with nature, dreams and sounds," and Krudewil, the realist, who examines one metaphor after another with unrelenting severity and humorous precision. At the end Krudewil takes two large balls of gray woolen yarn and knitting needles from his suitcase, and says: "Here, knit two, purl two. We're not going to talk any more about dreams. We're going to knit ourselves a new muse." "Well, what kind shall she be?" Pempelfort asks. Krudewil, the control figure in the borderland of that world in which objects appear now fantastic, now real, gives this answer to the romantic's question:

"Gray, mistrustful, without any botanical . . . knowledge of heaven and death, industrious, but deficient in the vocabulary of the erotic and completely void of dreams. . . . You know how I do it. . . . Before I write a poem I turn the light on and off three times. By this miracles are made impotent. . . . You've dropped a stitch. Be careful, Pem-

pelfort. Our new muse is a thrifty housekeeper. A faulty
upper part would displease her. She would dismiss us ruth-
lessly, have herself unraveled and knitted over again by a
machine."

Is this all there is to be said? Everything, certainly, that is strictly to the point and serves to
round off the matter humorously. But Grass, whose
favorite German author is Jean Paul Richter, adds a
flourish, a supplement sheet entitled, "Der Phantasie
gegenüber" [Regarding Imagination]. Bertolt Brecht,
practitioner of the stage, was fond of closing theoretical discussions with the sentence, "The proof of the
pudding is in the eating." Grass says: "Soft-boiled
eggs are best tested with the spoon." Wide-awake, the
poet sits "facing his imagination and considers all the
sentences and colons offered him, tests them with a
morose knocking like beating a teaspoon against an
egg." The poet is about to write a poem about a certain sort of close-netted wire fence. His table com-
panion, imagination, thinks that "the cosmos must
definitely be included. The motor elements of the net-
ted wire must swell to a staccato that transcends time
and the senses, is completely dissolved and blended
in new values. One can also change over from the
close-netted wire to the wire that is electrically
charged, symbolically grazing the barbed wire, and
in this way arrive at bold images, the most daring
associations, and an ending that is draped in death
and melancholy." The poet forbids himself cosmos,
barbed wire, and associations of death. He sticks to
the point, the close-netted product that he knows. He
gives up the poem which has not come off success-

fully. "Tomorrow he will try once again. Right after breakfast, teaspoon still in hand, sitting mistrustfully before blank paper, he will get the feeling of resistance, especially when an idea occurs to him."

Günter Grass will, one hopes, feel new resistance as he examines his old dramas and stronger resistance than heretofore as he drafts new ones. He will, one hopes, no longer tolerate "vacant passages" and the rather trite inversion of clichés, and also avoid the "tangibly dependable" criticized by Höllerer, "that has the ready phrase in stock and produces it." Thus far Grass's best work for the theater has been in the one-act play. As a scenic joke, as a paraphrase of the theme "the content as resistance," *Only Ten Minutes to Buffalo* is a showpiece of dramatic precision. Insofar as the world of art has consolidated itself in abstract art stereotypes, or hidden in them, or played dead, that world is, with the means of the theater of the absurd, recalled to life in this one-act play. In the one-act farce by Fritz Herzmanovsky-Orlando, *Kaiser Joseph und die Bahnwärterstochter* [Emperor Joseph and the Stationmaster's Daughter] the locomotive moves chugging *into* the picture. In Günter Grass it moves *out of* the picture; a real cowherd sets it properly in motion despite rust and abstract prases. Gazing after it in bewilderment are the painter Kotschenreuther (who sits on the flowery Bavarian meads contemplating cows and painting sailing ships), the atrociously overdressed lady, and the locomotive dilettantes Krudewil and Pempelfort, whose domicile is not reality. Wolfgang Hildesheimer sees in the "tiny

snapshot" made by this one-act play "a little diabol-
ical alarm ringing, a message, so to speak, about the
instability of the world"; Marianne Kesting says that
the play "draws its sustenance from its sheer imagistic effect."

In its economy of means, in the capacity of its
fantastic and realistic elements and their mutually
controlling contrasts, *The Flood* (published in the
edition Suhrkamp) is not quite so well-balanced a
play as the one we have just discussed. In the words
of Höllerer, it is, despite its two acts, a draft for a
one-act play. The action is left to one of the natural
elements—rain—and not to man. Günter Grass—
utilizer of wool-yarn remnants and thrifty knitter of
stockings for a gray muse—recites in Part Two of
the poem "The Flood" the proceedings on the stage:

> The cellar is under water, we have carried the crates up
> And are checking their contents against the list.
> So far nothing has been lost.
> Because the water is sure to go down soon,
> We have begun to sew parasols.
> It will be very difficult to cross the square again,
> Distinctly, with a shadow heavy as lead.
> We shall miss the curtain at first.
> And go into the cellar often
> To consider the mark
> That the water bequeathed to us.

The movement that in the poem carries effort-
lessly and almost unnoticed from line to line has to
be buttressed and strengthened on the stage. The
characters, who in the poem remain anonymous, in
the play are given names: Noah, a homeowner, his
sister-in-law Betty, his daughter Jutta, his son Leo.

In addition, there are Jutta's fiancé Henn and Leo's friend Kongo. Further, there are the philosophizing rats Strich and Perle (already mentioned) and "an examiner." Finally, there are stage props, including historic inkwells which Noah (who talks in a Biblical manner at times) collects. Out of the crates mentioned in the poem there issue contents that the poem did not mention: besides inkwells and chandeliers, preserve jars and photograph albums. Leo, who, with Kongo, steps out of one of the crates, says to Aunt Betty with friendly irony, "Anyone without a photo album is like a coffin without a lid." The props and the characters out of the crates stand around as part of the decoration. They talk and talk. Aunt Betty is sewing parasols out of parachute silk for the sunny days that are certainly coming after the flood. Daughter Jutta, the imaginative one, who is bored with her fiancé Henn, does a little fornicatting with Kongo. (Here there is Strindberg-type dialogue, doctored for laughs.) Meanwhile the water is rising. The rats talk in language that is poetic, destructive of meaning, laden with meaning, absurd. Aunt Betty sews parasols. And she is proved right: the water sinks, the joy of living rises, and the absurd rats leave the rescued house.

In a radio talk with Horst Bienek, Günter Grass once said: "Yes, my first prose ventures were a kind of salad made from Kafka and Ringelnatz, with a great many metaphors, so many that they were stepping on one another's tails. When I read them today I am astonished at how gifted I was then —and glad that they were not published."

The Flood was published. Deservedly, for it is on the whole a well-constructed play, with dialogue that is at time ingenious, entertaining, and poetic. Of course the props—inkwells and parasols—do not serve as other than a restorative joke about ineradicable restorative impulses on the brink of a catastrophe that is garnished with apocalyptic phrases. In some scenes, it appears to me, there are certain small vestiges of Grass's earliest attempts, samplings of what he called "a salad made from Kafka and Ringelnatz." Kafka could sign his name as architect (or auxiliary architect) of the house in the flood. The inkwell of Noah's collection in which the fugitive Queen Louise is supposed to have dipped her pen could have come from the posthumous papers of Joachim Ringelnatz.

But at the end, things in Grass do not, after all, turn out so untransparent and void of prospect as in Kafka, nor so steeped in childlike colors and so imaginative as in Ringelnatz. In the background stands Kurt Kusenberg and whispers to the rather pale creations on the stage, in the imitated voice of Axel Cäsar Springer: "Be nice to each other."

The Wicked Cooks is "a drama in five acts," and therefore more ambitious. In his excellent book, *The Theater of the Absurd*, M. Esslin says this "the most interesting of Günter Grass's plays" is "an ambitious attempt to make out of a religious reproach a poetic tragicomedy." The plot centers on the secret recipe for a gray soup that is seasoned with a certain pinch of ashes. The competing cooks —who move about the stage with sham merriment, with childlike grotesqueness and ballet-like buoy-ancy—intend to get the mysterious recipe out of the Count by every means of trickery and persua-sion, open and concealed threats, and blackmail. The Count (who was baptized with the plain name of Herbert Schymanski) is in love with the nurse Martha, and finally the cooks give him Martha for his wife, in return for which he is to give them the recipe. When the cooks Grün and Kletterer come to collect, the strange Count says: "I am sorry . . . I have told you often enough that there is no recipe, that it is an experience, a living knowledge, a mode of life. It should be known to you that no cook has ever yet succeeded in cooking the same soup twice." He adds that the last few months, his life with Martha, have made this experience superfluous: "I have forgotten it." But since he has broken his word by being unable to give the cooks the promised recipe, the Count and his wife Martha commit suicide.

The possibility of a confusing variety of inter-pretations is not something that dates just from the beginning of modern drama of the absurd, from Beckett and Ionesco. It can probably even be main-tained, and proved, that it is precisely this quality of manifold, contradictory, mutually canceling inter-pretations that belongs to the essence of the drama of the absurd. Nevertheless one should first of all ad-here to the text and read this text precisely to the end.

After the couple's suicide the cooks run away. To the question "Why?" the cook Grün replies: "The legs were the reason." The recipe was only a pretext. "It wasn't even the soup." While the cook Petri polishes the trumpet, cook Grün vanishes, saying, "I cannot like it here anymore." Cook Petri comments: "There he goes running. But in my legs, too, something is preparing for that, and wants to come closer to a goal that has been undertaken."

So the ultimate thing—in which sense and senselessness coincide—is movement, a running for running's sake, the course of the world? True, there is talk of a goal undertaken which one wants to come nearer to. But what goal is it? Here the dialectic of objects, the dialectic of content and form, seems to me to lead into a vacuum, or at least into something shapeless that cannot be visualized. About *The Wicked Cooks,* Marianne Kesting rightly objects that out of the choreographic and pantomimic images, crossed with realistic (and over-long) details, there could have been made perhaps a one-act piece but definitely not a full-length play. "An imagistic effect," she writes, "is by its very nature short and cannot be extended over several acts."

Besides this proof from stage practice, proof can also be demonstrated, on the basis of the double dialectic of content and form, that with *The Wicked Cooks* the dramaturgic possibilities that Grass has shown to date have reached a limit. This path led and leads no further. Let us recapitulate briefly. Content, congealing in the object, in the accessories of the stage, is for Grass neither allegory nor symbol in the old sense. Nevertheless the object is the meaning vehicle or form vehicle; or (more exactly) it becomes this in the course of the play. There are differences between the objects or accessories, differences between the revolver *(Mister, Mister),* the locomotive *(Only Ten Minutes to Buffalo),* the toothbrush *(Zweiunddreißig Zähne),* and the rising flood *(The Flood).*

The more or less tangible stage prop, the content, effects an artistic conquest of the resistance in more or less tangible forms. Here one might perceive a sequence of steps: revolver (object for murder), locomotive (object for motion), toothbrush (hygienic object), and flood (object or element of nature). In *The Wicked Cooks,* the sequence—from the readily visualized to the shapeless—reaches a height where the object itself, the soup recipe, disappears as the vehicle of resistance, dissolves into the abstract and the secret, and therefore can find answer and resistance only in a greater secret, the mystery of death. In no other play by Grass are there dead persons in whom the mystery of sacrifice is recognizable in the religious, Christian sense. To this extent Esslin might be correct in his interpretation after all.

The reservations and objections that arise sequentially in the act of critical analysis do not exist —at least they are not so clear-cut—in the sequential and/or simultaneous processes of the imagination. The imagination comprises more than the individual poem or drama is able to present. One must keep the entire creative process in mind and consider the fact that it takes place in greater breadth and intensity than is revealed in the finished product. Grass works a great deal and even doggedly on detail, and it is precisely with such an artist that impressions, experiences, and images which stimulate and excite his imagination are, for a time, consciously or unconsciously repressed. Then suddenly a figure will no longer be denied. All at once there are united in it things which have long been appearing in scattered rudiments and elements of lyric and drama, but which till now have been unable to attain that dynamism and carrying capacity which marks the great work, the "one chance in a million." That great work, which in some passages bears the stamp of genius, Günter Grass finally realized in his novel *The Tin Drum*. This novel cannot be understood without a knowledge of the elements and artistic forms developed by Grass in his lyrics and plays up to 1958. But neither can it be deduced from the knowledge of these elements and forms. A new and surprising flash of inspiration lit the spark.

5

Don't
Ask Oskar

In an interview published in the *Frankfurter Neue Presse* of November 14, 1959, Günter Grass said, in answer to the question as to how he had got the idea for the tin drummer:

"About seven years ago, at the home of friends of friends of mine, I saw a three-year-old boy with a tin drum hung around his neck. He was told to shake hands and say hello to the grown-ups, but he ignored them, wouldn't say hello to anybody, and kept to his drum. His point of view later became Oskar's point of view."

The question-and-answer session continued as follows:

"How did the material accumulate?"

"A good half of the material was always there. The other—equally good—half was furnished by Oskar with his 'point of view.' Any material in excess of the two good halves had to be stricken out."

"Did you intend from the very start to write a picaresque novel?"

"*The Tin Drum* is no more a picaresque novel—what is a picaresque novel?—than *Die Legende von Ulenspiegel und Lamme Goedzak* [The Legend of Ulenspiegel and Lamme Goedzak] is. The satire, the legend, the parable, the ghost story—everything, in short, that today is simply and simple-mindedly labeled surrealism—serve this reality and are part of it."

"What about the parallels that are often drawn with *Simplicissimus*? Are they justified? Did you have others for a model?"

"Certainly *The Tin Drum* may be traced to the adventurous *Simplicissimus,* certainly also to novels of individual development such as *Wilhelm Meister* and *Der grüne Hein-*

rich [Green Henry]. But the decisive influence for me was Herman Melville with his object mania, his *Moby Dick.*"

"How long did you work on *The Tin Drum*?"

"The first notes began in the summer of 1953. In February, 1959, the manuscript was completed."

"What difficulties with regard to form and content were there in the writing?"

"Because I excluded the use of flashbacks that is so popular today, things had to be told chronologically. That meant that I was always close to the material and a reality that had to be fixed and named exactly. So I needed voluminous chapter plans and timetables. Also, when one writes chronologically one has to be very industrious."

Grass makes very exact preliminary studies, similar to those that Thomas Mann used to make. The writing, (as Grass told a *Spiegel* editor) proceeds in three stages. In the first version, Grass records inspiration, memory, fancy. Then he fills in "gaps" with documentary material. Last, he polishes this second version until the inserted facts no longer seem like foreign matter.

In a radio talk with Horst Bienek (which the latter did *not* include in his collection *Werkstattgespräche mit Schriftstellern,* [Workshop Talks with Writers], Munich, 1962), Grass gave more precise information about his way of writing, especially in the field of the epic. From his answers it is clear that the two great novels, *The Tin Drum* and *Dog Years,* as well as the novella *Cat and Mouse,* can only be understood as parts of an encompassing whole. The center or core thereof, into which later events are projected and out of which they then unfold, is defined by the image world of early childhood and youth which Grass experienced in Danzig, the suburb Langfuhr, and the Vistula lowland. The content resists being formed until the right genre has been found, and the most suitable regulating energy in the principal and secondary characters, in the meter and rhythm, in the cadence of the dialogue. The author speaks without reluctance of the difficulties that can arise in doing this:

For a long time I tried to approach the whole complex of material of *The Tin Drum* by means of dialogue, but the material was too broad and flowed apart in all directions. The figure of Oskar Matzerath could not be made distinct by means of dialogue.

There were other preliminary stages of *The Tin Drum*. If one disregards the thirteen-year-old's attempt at novel writing (Grass set himself to write *Die Kaschuben* [The Cassubians] under the stimulus of a prize contest sponsored by *Hilf mit!*, the Nazi magazine for schools), a cycle of his poems is of particular note. Grass tells us:

About 1950-1951 I made my first trip to France, and there wrote a long, metaphor-laden, but not very good, cycle of poems called *Der Säulenheilige* [The Saint on the Column]. It tells about a young man, a mason—the time is today—who had suddenly had enough of life in the village and, with the help of his manual skill, built a column on which he sat and had his mother bring him his food on a pole. From that elevated perspective the young man (as I had planned it) described life in the village. At a later date, Oskar became the reverse of a saint on a column. It developed that the man on the column was too static for me to have him speak in prose, and for that reason Oskar came down from the column. He did not stay at normal height but came a little closer still to the earth, and then had a point of view the opposite of that of the saint on the column.

With the first sentence, with Oskar's confession —"I admit it: I am an inmate of a sanatorium and convalescent home"—the basic tone of the novel had been found. Out of the main figure, its peculiarity and its perspective, evolves the novel's over-all structure, often surprisingly for the author, and yet with inner consistency. Grass explains it as follows:

Only one character was definite. That was Oskar Matzerath and his development: that at the age of three he stops growing, at twenty-one, in accordance with normal development, decides to grow a bit, and gets a hump. And it was definite that the book would end with his thirtieth birthday.

The point of view from which Oskar sees the world makes it possible for Grass to describe people and events in a manner that neither children nor adults could observe and interpret. Oskar Matzerath acquires something of that now subhuman, now superhuman, power which formerly was attributed to figures of fairy tale and saga, demonic dwarfs, trolls, and giants transformed into toads. At the same time he remains—in a positively confounding way—natural, childlike, and naive. In the conversation with Bienek, Grass made reference to the consequences and the advantages resulting from the fact that his central character from the age of three grows no further, "but at the same time has from birth the intelligence and clear-sightedness of an adult, with all adult mistakes and false speculations; that, however, he is later not noticed by adults as an adult but remains always a little bit of a fellow; and that he sees everything constantly from this perspective looking upward from below, not only the people around him but the entire epoch."

Ernst Jünger once said that it is a characteristic of our time that the real is just as fantastic as the fantastic is real. And it was Friedrich Dürrenmatt who said that one cannot get at our epoch any longer with tragedy but only with comedy. With comedy in extreme form, the absurd drama and the grotesque. Both possibilities—which Grass, as we have shown, tested and played out in many forms in his poems and plays—unite and expand, with lyric and dramatic elements added, in his novels. Grass's predilection for the grotesque emerges in almost every scene, on almost every page of his works, in his (sometimes self-transforming) principal and secondary characters. This can be seen in the characterization of the dwarf drummer Oskar and his keeper Bruno (who makes plaster-coated figures of knotted string), of Joachim Mahlke with the oversized Adam's apple (*Cat and Mouse*), of Brauxel, alias Goldmäulchen, alias Eduard Amsel, who manufactures scarecrows (*Dog Years*). Even the *petit bourgeois* milieu in Danzig-Langfuhr and the artists' milieu in Düsseldorf—when seen through the eyes of the main character, the narrator—contain the possibility of describing a greater number of eccentrics than are generally portrayed in modern novels.

Grass makes use of the classically grotesque because therein, as he says, "everything, the tragic and the comic and the satiric, has room side by side and each supports the others." Oskar Matzerath, he says, remains a realistic figure and does not become a creature of artifice. In contrast to the at times unproductive, often merely mechanical, grotesqueness in the dramas (*Zweiunddreißig Zähne, The Wicked Cooks*), Grass in *The Tin Drum* succeeded in exploiting the possibilities of the classical grotesque. The dynamism that is in the drummer boy Oskar largely accords with Grass the narrator's own vitality. Grass's optics and the fact that Oskar is himself an eccentric make it certain that Oskar will discover an abundance of eccentrics round about him. The uniformity of modern mass society that has often been lamented by cultural critics and sociologists exists neither for Oskar Matzerath nor for Günter Grass. In the conversation with Bienek, Grass said:

The figures around Oskar Matzerath are mostly *petit bourgeois,* each of them—within the framework of the grotesque —an eccentric, or an "original," as one says in Germany. I think that we too are all eccentrics. The opinions, mostly deriving from sociologists, that deny the existence of the individual today and promote a pretty dismal uniformity—I don't see them proved. Even in a packed streetcar I do not see a mass of people; I see nothing but "originals," individual persons. One has a goiter, another has a big Adam's apple; one is big, another is small; one keeps blowing his nose and doesn't have a cold, another has a cold and doesn't blow his nose. . . .

In denying uniformity so vigorously, Grass contributes to overcoming the view (which has become almost a compulsive idea) that all processes in modern society are inevitable. In *The Tin Drum* the memoir-writing Oskar gives the following answer to the question, "How shall I begin?"

One can begin a story in the middle and stride boldly forward and boldly backward sowing confusion. One can be modern, eliminate all times and all distances, and afterwards announce or have it announced that one has, at last and in the nick of time, solved the space-time problem. One can also assert at the very beginning that today it is impossible to write a novel, and then—behind one's own back, so to speak —show one's ace with a smash hit, so as to end up as the last possible novelist. I have also had it said to me that it looks modest and nice to assert in the beginning that there are no heroes in novels anymore because there are no individualists anymore, because individuality has been lost, because man is solitary, everyone alike is solitary, without the right to individual solitariness, and forms a nameless and heroless solitary mass. All that may be true in its way. But speaking for myself, Oskar, and for my keeper Bruno, I would like to state: We are both heroes, quite different heroes, he behind the peephole, I in front of it, and when he opens the door the two of us, with all our friendship and all our loneliness, still are not a nameless and heroless mass.

One should not draw false conclusions from this oft-quoted passage. It has the ring of a pronunciamento, and in polemically pointed negative terms contains what is almost like an artistic program, a theory of the novel. But one should be wary of pushing this utterance too far or making it into an absolute. It is impossible to miss the ironic and self-ironic inflection, in which there is expressed an attitude of distance. Oskar Matzerath sets this note of distance even when he yields the floor to other speakers—his keeper Bruno or the impresario Gottfried von Vittlar (who at his own wish reports him to the police) and lets them do the narrating.

The furious quality of some chapters, in which the narrator seems to yield the conduct of the narrative to his drum, the amplitude of the figures, and the many fantastic-grotesque scenes, all could easily, in a first reading of *The Tin Drum*, give rise to the impression of an overflowing and in part undisciplined manner of narrative. This impression does not stand critical scrutiny. To be sure there are weak, or rather weak, lackluster passages, especially in Book Three; at times there are distracting repetitions and witticisms; and at several points one could do without the distasteful exactitude. Nevertheless, even in those sections which are open to criticism in their details, the tone of distance set by the main character (in lessened degree) is artistically maintained. If this note of distance becomes altered to such an extent that it can no longer come within Oskar's field of vision, a new figure and a new perspective appears. If its problem gains so much specific gravity as to require a separate presentation, it is lifted out. This is what took place during the writing of *The Tin Drum* at the appearance of Joachim Mahlke (the central figure of the novella *Cat and Mouse*). In the composition of *Dog Years* also, the note of distance among the three respective narrators, and between each narrator and the events he is relating, is exactly defined.

From the epic works and personal statements of Günter Grass, his creative process can be discerned pretty clearly. The foundation is that which he experienced with all his senses in early childhood and youth against the backdrop of Danzig, the Vistula lowland, and West Prussia—an inexhaustible

reserve of materials, characters, gestures, and shad-
ings of speech. Some of it finds expression in a form
to which the term autobiographic, in its usual sense,
does not apply. Grass has therefore opposed the
assertion that his epic works are to be regarded as
more or less veiled autobiographies. He has said:

So far as I can recall my own life, I find passages from it
neither in *The Tin Drum* nor in the novella *Cat and Mouse*.
I do not intend to write something autobiographical, nor do
I believe it possible. On the other hand there are naturally
hints of things remembered, in a word, an odor, a touch, in
something I only heard tell of—and these things, these fragments of experiences can be recast much more easily in a
short story. In addition there is the fact that every book in its
entirety—including secondary figures, landscape, selection
and choice of theme—is naturally a piece of the author, a
defined piece, and also signifies a self-discovery on the part
of the author.

Grass went on to say that he saw no reason to
change the scene of his writings during the next
twenty years. He is very familiar, he said, with the
suburb Langfuhr, which has about 75,000 inhabi-
tants, and with all its streets, side streets, squares,
and out-of-the-way corners, and is able to write
many novels yet, one for each of the fifteen or six-
teen city districts. "In short, with Langfuhr, the
mouth of the Vistula, the port area, the bathing
resorts, Zoppot and its vicinity, the Cassubian-
Polish part, and West Prussia generally, I am working at full capacity."

The image world of Günter Grass's childhood
and youth which he has absorbed and developed
should not—despite the many details captured with

surprising precision—be imagined as something static. It rests, like Vineta, on the sea bottom of memory. ("Danzig *Plattdeutsch*," Grass has said, "is to me what Latin is to a high-school teacher. It is a dying language.") At the same time life in and around Danzig goes on. Grass perceives this. Düsseldorf and Berlin and other large cities seem to him like suburbs of the suburb Langfuhr. Grass, however, also knows at first hand the Danzig of today with its Polish population. Thus in his novels the arc extends from Danzig's early history, by means of the Danzig he knew in his youth, to the present day. Unprejudiced and without resentment he sees the new generation of sixteen- and seventeen-year-olds in Zoppot and the present-day population of his native city:

I have been struck by the fact that the people who live in Danzig come mostly from Vilna and Bialystok, from the flat country and not from the seacoast. And yet on the banks of the Modlau—that is a tributary of the Vistula which flows through Danzig—I have seen men who have the rolling gait which really belongs only to people who were born in a port city. It may be that something such as this helps to form human nature and that this is a factor which transcends nationalities.

The homeland of West Prussia lives in Grass's books, yet there is in them not a trace of narrow regionalism or provincialism; there is no resentment, no idealizing or false romanticism, no incipient hardening of any kind into nationalism or ideology. Nevertheless, or perhaps for this very reason, Danzig, the German Danzig, is described so exactly and so truly to nature that it could be reconstructed in a model like the Lübeck of the Buddenbrooks or the Berlin of the transport worker Franz Biberkopf.

"On a future map of world literature, it is possible that Danzig may be marked as a place just as important as Joyce's Dublin or Kafka's Prague." This speculation was expressed by Thomas von Vegesack in an article on Grass in the *Stockholms Tidningen* of November 20, 1961. Some critics passionately disputed it; others, with more or less good arguments, proclaimed it as a certainty. In the pros and cons of debates over the worth or lack of worth of Günter Grass as a writer, agreement or assimilation of differing judgments is not to be expected soon. A prerequisite for adequate critical evaluation is a precise definition of standpoint, a clear distinction between the perspective of the author and the first-person narrator or team of narrators (Oskar Matzerath in *The Tin Drum*, Pilenz in *Cat and Mouse,* and the trio Amsel, Liebenau, and Matern in *Dog Years*). From this perspective (or these perspectives)—now coinciding, now only appearing to coincide, now clearly diverging—the relation between man and object is seen and examined. The part played by the emotional and irrational is revealed and diminished. A demon is exorcised.

The best start toward an analysis of Günter Grass's style has been made by Klaus Wagenbach in an essay about Grass which appears in *Schriftsteller der Gegenwart/Deutsche Literatur: Dreiundfünfzig Porträts* [Present-Day Writers: German Literature,

Fifty-Three Portraits], (edited by Klaus Nonnenmann, Olten and Freiburg im Breisgau, 1963). As
the three most important characteristics of Grass as
a writer, Wagenbach lists: syntactic articulation, perspective, and treatment of time: "The narrator takes
his time. Characteristics, object and activities are
presented to the reader by means of pictorial variation that always causes the same word to dance as if
positively hypnotized." Wagenbach speaks of an
"artistic stuttering rhythm, a leitmotif-like persis-
tence in detail." There is, he says, an "object compulsion." The objects make themselves independent,
they gain a magic of their own (like the drum), they
become a fetish (like the galleon figure):

The objects, always with new verbs, are ruled as it were by
an object. In this way all discrimination of an object by a
subject is eliminated; the things remain among themselves.
This is a proof of not only the nonmoral narrative attitude
but also the nonaesthetic point of view. To measure such a
text by such categories as disgust or rapture, ugliness or
beauty, is hardly possible. That would presuppose an
(engaged) subject, which in this case does not appear at all.

What follows from this? An exclusion of
ethics? Indifference and inhumanity?

In a third section entitled "Revidierte Zeit"
["Time under Review"], Klaus Wagenbach examines
the organizing principle that underlies the entire
structure.

The techniques that we have described—time under the
magnifying glass, cumulative detail, object compulsion—are
regulated in themselves; they lead either to the "small form"
or to epic extravagance. For this reason Grass's epic works

are more rigorously constructed than are those of most of his contemporaries, not only within the framework of the powerful narrative but also by means of a very careful time framework.

By means of associations, anticipations, and corrections, the narrator constantly re-examines the distance between the time when he is narrating and that time in the past which is the subject of his narration. Toward the end (in *The Tin Drum* as well as in *Cat and Mouse* and *Dog Years*) this distance steadily diminishes. In the alternation between the onward march of the narrative and the pause to take the snapshot of the image, doubts are awakened:

The alternation serves the purpose of mutual revision. Grass is also a revisionist vis-à-vis the object. If a moralistic tendency is recognizable anywhere in his works, it is in this technique of manifold refraction. Things remain among themselves, and yet are narrated. The narrator narrates, and yet acknowledges an "author, who invented us for professional reasons" (*Cat and Mouse*). The reader seemingly remains excluded, and yet is addressed with the words "You who have to lead a confused life" (*The Tin Drum*). Time is in flux, and yet is cemented in paradigms. This constant alternation also conveys to the reader the feelings of reserve, of great mistrust, of radical doubt.

In the exact and mistrustful examination of the relationships, in the radical doubt, in the call for what Klaus Wagenbach describes as "general ideological disinfection," there is no denial of humanity and morality but rather the realization resulting from painful experience that an age of inhumanity, in order to be fully understood, cannot and must not be portrayed with the old familiar stylistic means.

"God is a bad stylistic principle," Gottfried Benn once said. Humanity and morality too are, in certain circumstances, bad stylistic principles. When human beings become human material, become objects, the appeal to humanity is insufficient to liberate them from this servitude. A dictatorship of objects is needed, a tyranny of the drum, before the demon can be exorcised. *The Tin Drum* offers many examples of the success and failure of such frivolous infantile attempts. Let us cite one gay example that has become famous: the grotesque scene in which the boy Oskar, crouching under the speakers' platform of a National Socialist Party rally on the Maiwiese in Danzig, coaxes the crowd to fall under his spell by virtuoso use of his drum:

The drum lay before me, already in position. Lovely and loose I let the sticks play in my hands and, with tenderness in my wrists, laid an artistic and gay waltz tempo on my drum, letting it grow louder, more intense, conjuring Vienna and the Danube, until overhead the first and second troopers' drums took a liking to my waltz and the side drums of the older boys, more or less skillfully, took up my overture. In between, it's true, there were the inflexible ones with no sense of hearing who went on beating boom-boom, and boom-boom-boom, when I meant the three-quarter time that the people love so well. Oskar was about to despair, then the fanfare trumpets began to get the idea, and the fifes, oh Danube, piped so blue. Only the leaders of the trumpeters and drummers didn't believe in the Waltz King and shouted their annoying commands, but I had deposed them. This was now my music. And the people thanked me. Laughter got loud in front of the platform, then some were singing along, oh Danube, and across the whole field, so blue, as far as Hindenburgallee, so blue, and to Steffenspark,

so blue, my rhythm went skipping, reinforced by the micro-
phone over me turned up to full volume. I peered out
through my knothole—but still kept busily drumming—and
saw that the people enjoyed my waltzes, skipped in excite-
ment, had it in their legs. Nine couples and now another
couple were dancing, mated by the Waltz King. The only
one that the waltz time didn't suit was Löbsack. With district
Party chiefs and SA battalion leaders, with Forster, Greiser
and Rauschning, with a long brown tail end of party official-
dom, he stood in the middle of the crowd, boiling as the
passage through to the platform began to close in front of
him. He was used to being steered to the platform to the
tune of straight march music. These frivolous sounds made
him lose his faith in the people.

SA and SS men search for the mischief-maker
under the platform. "They did not find Oskar, because he was too much for them." Comparison with
the prophet Jonah is resisted, and also God's anger
threatening Nineveh, "even when it was called Danzig." Also refused is the world outlook that cuts
heroes and saints like stencils while it makes human
beings into human material and without scruple is
just as ready to use them as "fuel" for its ends as it is
to transform them: "My drum was not Biblical, so I
stuck it under my pullover, I had enough to do with
myself; without bumping myself I found my way out
of the bowels of an all-purpose rostrum which only
by chance had the proportions of a prophet-
devouring whale."

A significant characteristic of Grass is the
value-free sphere into which he leads his drummer
again and again, the swing back into a dismal everyday state after the wild unbridled movement. Oskar

—who himself does evil, tempts others to evil, and who nevertheless resists the manifestations of power and of evil as they appear in the spirit of the age—at the same time brings about by his presentation of events a recognition of the special, twilight-lit enigmatic character of evil, its banality which appears in the most remarkable crossbreeds of kindness and crime, musical ear and pathological urge to murder. In *The Tin Drum* this theme is played through in many variations, with special impressiveness and art of a high order in the chapter, "Faith, Hope, Charity." In this chapter the keeper comes to Oskar's bed, takes his patient's hands away from the drum and says: "But Herr Matzerath, if you keep on drumming so loudly, people elsewhere will hear that there is much too loud drumming here. Won't you take a pause or drum a little softer?" Oskar is willing. He decides to dictate a new, softer chapter to his drum. But it is in this very chapter that the only friend he has had in his life, the Jewish toy dealer Markus from Danzig, dies in the *Kristallnacht* of the year 1938. Oskar knows a couple of those who are guilty of his death. The SA man Meyn, who plays the trumpet so beautifully, is one of these guilty ones. And so at the end, with a hard drum roll, Oskar dictates these sentences of reminiscence:

There was once a tin-drum player named Oskar, and they took from him his toy dealer.

There was once a toy dealer named Markus, and he took all the toys out of the world with him.

There was once a musician named Meyn, and if he is not dead he is still living and again plays the trumpet beautifully.

Like the dismal everyday state of things, so too evil remains in the world. Murder does not die with the murderer; tyranny does not die with the death of the tyrant. Guilt also remains. It seeks and finds places to hide. And it is roused by fear. Fear is here projected into the shadow figure of "a child's bogieman that keeps getting blacker." This shadow figure saw from the earliest days what no human being noticed and what conscience would like to deny and the drum would like to drown out. The Black Cook of German nursery rhymes—is she a phantom or a reality? Is she a thing born of fear and guilt or an emissary of infernal or celestial powers? Is she life? Is she death?

"Don't ask Oskar. He can't find another word."

6

For What Began
with Cat
and Mouse

On September 28, 1962, a motion was made by an office in the Ministry of Labor, Health, and Welfare of the state of Hesse that the novella *Cat and Mouse,* by Günter Grass, be included in the list of writings dangerous to youth. This motion (initiated without the knowledge of Minister Heinrich Hemsath and soon thereafter withdrawn by him) read in part as follows:

The work contains numerous descriptions of obscenities which are apt to morally endanger children and adolescents. Reference is made to pages 28, 38–43, 53, 54, 98, 102, 104, 112, 130, 139, and 140. The passages objected to, which included detailed scenes of that kind with emphatic complete-ness, are strewn throughout the story without any recog-nizable purpose. The manner of these presentations allows the conclusion that they have been included only because of their obscene attraction. They are apt to encumber nega-tively the imagination of adolescent readers, arouse them to sexual actions and thereby impair their upbringing. They are therefore in no sense to be reconciled with the purpose of the author as indicated on the dust jacket. The content of the story has for its subject the life and activities of a second-year high-school class in Danzig during World War II. At the center stands the hero—who it would be correct to say has been elevated by his comrades as an idol—Big Mahlke, whose especially prominent Adam's apple, as "an attribute of masculinity, precocious masculinity," becomes "the cause of all the boys' deeds, the mainspring of his career . . . even to the point of winning a high war decoration." Within this framework the descriptions of individual, more or less banal, matters, which incidentally display exclusively nega-tive symptoms, are deserving of particular literary interest neither in style nor content. Although perhaps it cannot be denied that the author has a certain ability and a certain style of writing, his book cannot from any standpoint be evaluated as being of service to art within the sense of Article 1, Paragraph 2, Law for Protection of Juveniles.

This document could be left to rest in the obscurity of a file cabinet as a testimonial to bureaucratic narrow-mindedness. But I believe that the adverse reactions it produced can serve to reduce, if not to eliminate, at least some of the prejudices about the alleged immorality or obscenity of Günter Grass that continue to exist among the public. About the document (soon withdrawn), the following writers and literary historians of note have made statements: Professor Fritz Martini, Professor Walter Jens, Dr. H. C. Kasimir Edschmid, and Dr. Hans Magnus Enzensberger. Their expert reports contain reasoned arguments refuting the motion. More convincing than these, however, is the comprehensive scientific rebuttal undertaken by the certified psychologist Dr. Emil Ottinger. His report (printed in full in the *Eckart Jahrbuch*, 1964-1965, Witten and Berlin, 1964) begins with the statement: "The novella *Cat and Mouse* is the story of a high-school student and the road he is destined to travel to maturity. It is gripping in its truth: biological, legislative, psychological."

Dr. Ottinger is also the author of an article entitled "Zur mehrdimensionalen Erklärung von Straftaten Jugendlicher am Beispiel der Novelle *Katz und Maus* von Günter Grass [Toward a Multi-dimensional Explanation of Punishable Offenses by Adolescents, with Examples Taken from Günter Grass's Novella *Cat and Mouse*] (in the *Monatsschrift für Kriminologie und Strafrechtsreform*, Vol. 5/6, 1962, pages 175–183). In his expert's report he arrives at the following conclusion: "In reading the novella, the penal lawyer, the psychiatrist, the court physician, the criminologist, all are concerned, each with regard to his special field; they find their scientific perceptions confirmed and artistically concentrated." Each of the passages that were objected to in the novella is examined with precision. The psychologist asks with justice: "If the authors of the motion find 'obscene attractions' in certain passages of the novella, is this proof that these passages 'negatively encumber the imagination of adolescent readers'? Can it not be asserted much more readily that, as a result of the author's drastic realism, of his apt, idiomatic narrative style, the sexual sphere is divested of everything dark and dim, everything lubricious, sultry and stifling, and thus that the ugliness of naked impulse is displayed to the adolescent reader, thereby producing a repelling reaction that from the standpoint of sexual morality is desirable?"

Especially noteworthy is, as Dr. Ottinger writes, "the unawareness, on the part of the authors of the motion, of the growing problem of an epochal biological phenomenon that for decades has been a source of increasing concern to the societies of all civilized nations: the problem of acceleration, the partial acceleration of the maturing process in adolescents."

At the close of his very thorough report, Dr. Ottinger explains the fate of the high-school boy Joachim Hahlke whom Grass has portrayed; he does it from the standpoint of a scientist who is as knowledgeable as he is sensitive:

Mahlke's biological precocity it striking. That is a biological encumbrance. He becomes isolated because he no longer agrees with the behavior of his age peers. That is an emotional encumbrance. Others show hostility toward him because his being different provokes the collective group. That is a sociopsychological encumbrance. Because of his natural tendency he must make strenuous and exaggerated attempts to compensate. That is a constitutional encumbrance. He falls into a state of continuing and perverse compulsive seeking for compensation. That is a neurotic encumbrance. He tries to solve the neurotic encumbrance by aggression. This leads to moral encumbrance, after his society has become a repressive one. Rehabilitation from emotions and their lasting aftereffects is denied him. This becomes an existential encumbrance. Grass has exposed this whole process in the fictional narrative of a life.

When he shows with deeply moving effect how an adolescent's will to survive breaks under the weight of this accumulated encumbrance, then this novella is of service to art because it is of service to that truth which we are able to see at the present stage of our knowledge of adolescent nature. The art of this novella consists of concentrating the experience and intuition which, in their separate areas, are possessed respectively by high-school teachers, psychiatrists specializing in the problems of youth, constitutional biologists, juvenile court judges, criminological sociologists, youth counselors and psychologists. To give this artistic concentration compelling force, Grass goes into detail. It is the best of artistic and psychological methods to accord full rank to that fact which is easily overlooked.

To call shocking details shocking is part of the social function of aggressive literature. Grass does not attack adolescent morality but rather that adult society which, inhibited by taboos, does not see its profound co-responsibility for the fate of youth. He who seeks to discover where this co-responsibility lies will read with pensiveness these words at the end of the novella: "For what began with cat and mouse, tortures me today. . . ."

So much for the expert report of Emil Ottinger.

With cat and mouse the novella begins, as the narrator Pilenz sets a black cat upon the "mouse"—the oversized Adam's apple of the sleeping ball-player, who is his schoolmate Mahlke. Only late in the story is its narrator presented in his own sphere of activity:

I, Pilenz—what does it matter, my first name—former altar boy, wanted to become I don't know what all, now secretary in the Catholic Welfare house, can't keep away from magic. I read Bloy, the Gnostics, Böll, Friedrich Heer, and, often disconcerted, good old St. Augustine's *Confessions;* I debate for nights on end over cups of too-black tea the blood of Christ, the Trinity, and the sacrament of grace with Father Alban, an open-minded, halfway believing Franciscan. I tell him of Mahlke and Mahlke's virgin, of Mahlke's gullet and Mahlke's aunt, of the part down the middle of Mahlke's head, of sugar-water, phonograph, snowy owl, screwdrivers, bundles of wool ends, light buttons, of cat and mouse and *mea culpa.* . . .

Once again the author's high level of artistic understanding is seen in the fact that he sets a distance between himself and the first-person narrator which makes it possible for him to portray the events close up, through the medium of one who feels himself guilty—and, at the same time, to objectify those events by quietly and (so to speak) indirectly exposing them to examination. In his talk with Horst Bienek, Grass emphasized the fact that the heroes of his novels always have a stimulus when they are first-person narrators: "Oskar has his drum, and Pilenz the altar boy has a guilt complex. That for him provides the impulse to write the story of Mahlke."

Here too, then, there is distance, the endeavor to create a value-free sphere in which all events are represented insofar as they can be rationally interpreted and realistically comprehended, but at the same time—by just this special utilization of the first-person narrator—the indissoluble secret of life and death is preserved. In the secret chapel of Mary that Mahlke has built to the Mother of God in the radio cabin of the wreck, he finally disappears. His disappearance does not lessen the surrounding world's share of guilt. But even with this shared guilt—that which the narrator attributes to himself, and that which the reader may more or less strongly feel—the poetic content and the spiritual substance that the novella contains are not exhausted. The quality of having several levels of meaning, a quality inherent in the creations of Günter Grass, finds particularly clear expression in a passage that Karl Korn has called "the core of the novella":

Actually—later rumors and definite facts to the contrary—for Mahlke, if there was to be a woman at all, it was only the Catholic Virgin Mary. It was only because of her that he dragged into the chapel of Mary everything that could be worn and shown on the neck. Everything he did, from diving to his later military achievements, he did for her, or rather—at once I must contradict myself—to divert attention from his Adam's apple. Finally—without Virgin and mouse losing their validity—a third motif can be named: our high school, that stuffy box that could not be ventilated, and especially its auditorium, meant much to Joachim Mahlke, and later compelled you to make the ultimate effort.

7

Each
of Us Bathes
by Himself

At first there were outlines, drafted and redrafted versions, revisions in perspective and time framework. The novel did not have the title *Dog Years* in the beginning. On the occasion of a visit by the Swiss author Hugo Loetscher at the beginning of 1960, Grass said that he was working on a novel "that takes for its theme the clichés of fascism, communism, and democracy—in other words a political novel, but a novel and not politics. Not the compensation idea and not the Atomic Club. Not the noble and beautiful Jewess and the beastly National Socialist, not the housebroken democrats and the unhousebroken Communists, but a novel of projected ideas and projected characters for which the model is the ambivalence, the ambiguity of our age" (*du, Kulturelle Monatsschrift,* June 1960, page 20).

At the Aschaffenburg meeting of the Gruppe 47, Günter Grass read a chapter from a new novel entitled *Kartoffelschalen* [Potato Peelings]. The chapter told the story of Hitler's shepherd dog who, surviving his master, crosses over from Ulbricht's Germany into the Federal Republic of West Germany. The "potato peelings" leitmotif was later rejected. (Grass says: "The peelings became too long.") By July, 1963, the novel *Dog Years* was published in its entirety. Like Böll's *The Clown,* it became a best-seller of 1963 and the following season.

The critic Klaus Wagenbach has spoken of the "artistic stuttering rhythm" of Günter Grass. *Dog Years* too is composed with virtuosity in stuttering rhythm. Only in appearance does Grass distribute the voluminous writing task among a collection of three authors: a radio author named Harry Liebenau, the miller's son Walter Matern, and Brauxel. Brauxel, who is not so particular about the way his name is written, asserts at the very beginning (in Book One, subtitled *Frühschichten*): "Playfulness and pedantry do not contradict each other; each dictates the other." This dictum is also valid for the author Grass, who splits himself up, as it were, into three self-invented ghostwriters, without at any point sacrificing his originality, his grandiose and whimsical ingenuity, or the rhythm of his language. In artistically precipitate stuttering rhythm, the novel begins:

You tell. No, you tell. Or you. Should the actor begin? Or the scarecrows, every which way? Or do we want to wait until the eight planets have made conjunction in the sign of Aquarius? Please, you begin. After all, it was your dog. But before my dog it was your dog and the dog's dog. Somebody has to begin: You or He or You or I. . . . Many, many sunsets ago, long before we were, the Vistula flowed, day in day out, without reflecting us and kept emptying always.

In comparison with *The Tin Drum, Dog Years* marks a loss and a gain. A loss not of the center, but of that one central figure who forces everything into his drum rhythm, Oskar Matzerath. In the new novel, despite the oft-repeated assertion that "the dog is central," there is no such dominantly impressive figure. But there was probably no other way of actualizing the theme Grass had chosen, the representation of present-day society in a kind of imaginary historiography. Thus the novel *Dog Years,* after the strict novella form used in *Cat and Mouse,*

marks a gain, above all in the enlargement and re-
finement of the narrative technique. The execution
of the theme sounded in the opening paragraph
demonstrates the high level of the author's artistic
understanding.

Three persons tell, each from his own point of
view, the story of the Führer's dog Prinz, around
which the so-called world history and world-war
history groups itself in stories. The nucleus, the dog
story, is related in a cadence that is a mild parody of
the Bible:

There was once a dog named Perkun, who belonged to a
Lithuanian miller's man, who had found employment at the
mouth of the Vistula. Perkun survived the miller's man and
sired Senta. The bitch Senta, who belonged to a miller in
Nickelswalde, whelped Harras. Harras, the male dog, who
belonged to a master cabinetmaker in Danzig-Langfuhr,
covered the bitch Thekla, who belonged to a Herr Leeb, who
died at the beginning of 1942 shortly after the bitch Thekla
died. The dog Prinz, sired by the male German shepherd
Harras and whelped by the bitch German shepherd Thekla,
made history: he was presented as a gift to the Führer and
Reich Chancellor, became his favorite dog, and got into the
weekly newsreel.

The concise references to Prinz's ancestors,
and to the scarecrows as the static figures, the inclusion of the Vistula (in the opening passage just
cited) as a river of time that flows through and beyond the dog years, denote with poetry and sufficient exactness the system of coordinates within
which the fable is unwound. The fable, in the nar-
rower sense of the word, comprises a section of German history, the most recent past, the time from

1935 to 1955. The fable, recited in three books—
Book One "Frühschichten" [Early Morning Shifts];
Book Two, "Liebesbriefe" [Love Letters]; Book
Three, "Materniaden" [Materniads]—by three narrators (Brauxel, Liebenau, and Matern) is com-
prised of fragments. Fragments of the history of the
German colonization of Eastern Europe, especially
in the lowland of the Vistula; fragments of family
histories and genealogies; fragments of a three-
sectioned novel of individual development. Fitted
into the composition are numerous episodes,
anecdotes, picaresque tales, tall stories, grotesque
creations, satires, even discussions of current issues
(for example, in the form of a radio feature, a kind
of Faustian parody of the unbased and insubstantial
mania for discussion that exists in our day). One
could name other elements of this novel, which
is created with artistry, indeed with virtuosity—
elements such as the inclusion of historical docu-
ments, newspaper reports, and classified advertise-
ments, and especially the parody of the conceptual
language of the philosopher Martin Heidegger. In
continuing the stylistic experiments of Expression-
ism and Dadaism in a way that is completely his
own, Grass is attempting by means of parody to
arrive at a new form of structure in the novel. In
some sections at the close of Book Two "Liebesbriefe" he succeeds brilliantly, in others he succeeds
satisfactorily, and in still others he does not succeed.

Infectious in its simplicity is the fable that is
the nucleus of the book: the story of the shepherd
dog Prinz, who before the outbreak of World War II

is presented by the party leadership of the Danzig District to the Führer and Reich Chancellor Adolf Hitler. Grass does not tell the story from the dog's perspective. Such a (basically unrealistic) presentation, although it might produce many transient effects, would shift the novel's theme—the fate and guilt of human beings in the recent past—onto the level of the instinctive and the irrational; it would upgrade the out-of-date fable of collective guilt and transfer it to recesses in which the responsibility and the failure of the individual could no longer be ascertained.

Grass simplifies by differentiating. And what has been simplified by differentiation he further differentiates. He has evolved his own variety of dialectic. He invents scarecrows in order to break the dictatorship of scarecrows, i.e., of ideologies. The novel *Dog Years* offers, after Brecht and Dürrenmatt, a fresh start in the German language toward grasping a reality that eludes the traditional realistic style of writing just as it does the experimental effort that is undertaken without passion for or gift in narrative. Grass is master, at times with an almost terrifying virtuosity, of an abundance of stylistic devices. He employs them, untroubled by the limits imposed by morality and taste. Occasionally he overestimates the language's endurance capacity, but he seldom falls into the error of pursuing artistry in language for its own sake. He keeps returning to the everyday world, to the earth, to the bank of the Vistula, and to the eccentrics of his homeland who have been transplanted to the West. Many readers of *Dog Years* have already made friends with these eccentrics: with the student Eddi Amsel, who makes scarecrows; his friend, the miller's son Walter Matern, and his father, who prophesies from flour sacks (and who after 1945 was consulted also by the superstitious publisher Axel Springer); the high-school teacher Brunies, who sucks cough drops, and later vitamin C tablets; his adopted child Jenny, the sensitive ballet dancer; and, above all, Grandmother Matern, who is like a figure from the world of the Eddas transported to Masurian country. Readers of *Dog Years* already know these figures as they know figures from the novels of Wilhelm Raabe and Thomas Mann. These readers shudder at the name of Tulla Prokriefke—how coarse is the behavior of this gaunt beast, who sets in front of the boy a decoction of leech soup. In this novel too there are many coarse and nauseating escapades and blasphemous and obscene episodes. It is as if the Danzig author had his miller's son Matern say: "I'll go Henry Miller one better."

One can reject some of these scenes. One can also raise the question as to whether anti-Semitism and the persecution and extermination of the Jews ought to be treated in the way that Grass treats them. Stylistic deficiencies can be censured. Polemics can be developed against the mixing of sex and politics. Grass parodies the language and the ideas of Heidegger, and it can be asked whether he has refuted Heidegger's world by his construction and thereby overcome it from within. This question becomes acute in the public radio debate with Walter

Matern. The chorus of debaters shouts: "Heidegger ho, Heidegger hum! The question is, Do you believe in God?" Walter Matern is evasive. He answers with Heidegger quotations that the strictest of the debate participants does not accept as valid. Since only a clear yes or no is admissible, Matern finally replies to the question, "Do you believe in God?" with: "Well . . . (a pause) . . . In the name of the Trinity: no."

The question left open is whether this answer of Walter Matern is to be equated with the answer of Günter Grass. What is definite is that to the following question by Walter Matern, "Who is directing here, holds the strings in his hand, who?" the discussion leaders in their turn give an evasive and unsatisfactory answer. Other questions besides this one remain open. And yet an answer is given, an answer in pictures. In the closing chapter Grass tells of a visit to a strange underground factory, half potash plant, half clothing factory, in which scarecrows of all kinds are produced. This underworld, which one should not be too quick to call a hell or a modern counterpart to Dante's Inferno, is a satiric likeness of what today we are fond of calling the pluralistic society. Just beneath the factory roof are a few dozen rooms, which are grippingly described in their weirdness and precision, even if overloaded with symbolic content. In these rooms the ideological scarecrows of our day are produced. At the end of the visitors' tour, the word is: "Orcus is up above." Ascending alone in the cable car, Brauxel and Matern reach daylight. "Twilight creeps from the Harz across the land."

The novel closes with these words:

And this man and that man—who will now call them Brauxel and Matern?—I and he, we stride with lamps extinguished to the storeroom, where the attendant takes our helmets and carbide lamps. I and he are led by the attendant to cabins, where Matern's and Brauxel's clothes have been kept. He and I step out of our miner's togs. For me and him bathtubs have been filled. I hear Eddi splashing next door. Now I step into my bath. The water leaches the dirt off us. Eddi is whistling something indefinite. I try to whistle something similar. But it's hard. We're both naked. Each of us bathes by himself.

8

. . . Is a Fool
and Changes
the World

With the four-act play *The Plebeians Rehearse the Uprising* (1966), Günter Grass, whose pursuit of his goals is as deliberate as it is tenacious, achieved something that his previous plays had either not done or had done only rarely. The play was booked for additional runs. In a radio talk with Hans Mayer and Marcel Reich-Ranicki, he said that his "German tragedy" had "endurance." And it does indeed have "endurance." Staged by Hansjörg Utzerath, it had its premiere in Berlin. In June, 1966, it was performed at the Ruhr Festival, where it produced a more balanced effect and received greater applause from the audience and critics. Soon the play was seen in Braunschweig and Karlsruhe, in the Burgtheater in Vienna, and at the festival held in the cloister ruin at Bad Hersfeld. With this play, which treats of the events of June 17, 1953, in East Berlin, Grass sought and found a new point of approach. He turned to the reality of divided Germany. Grass, who has lived in West Berlin since 1960, sees the above-mentioned reality very soberly, yet not without an *engagement* that can be exactly defined. This *engagement*—which, notwithstanding his preference for the Social Democratic Party, never finds merely uncritical expression—draws quite a sharp distinction between art and politics from the start, and therefore avoids dangers and escapes compromises that can easily be fatal for *engagé* writers.

A comparison of Grass's fundamental essay "Der Inhaltals Widerstand" (of 1957) with the address he delivered in April, 1966, at Princeton University "Vom mangelnden Selbstvertrauen der schreibenden Hofnarren unter Berüchsichtigung nicht vorhandener Höfe [On the lack of Self-Confidence of the Literary Court Jester Without a Court] (printed in the periodical *Akzente,* Vol. 3, June, 1966) clearly shows the artist Grass's consistency in thought and action, and how this view was confirmed by his political experiences in the West German Bundestag election campaign in the summer of 1965. To the cliché of a utopia of yesterday, which (in his opinion) is expressed in the political engagement of the author Peter Weiss, he opposes a different, discriminating view—or, if you will, utopia. The politically alert writer must perform a double function. As an artist he must, on the one hand, remain a fool in order to be able to write uncompromisingly. If, however, he is one of those authors who "on occasion leave their desks and deal in the small change of democracy," he must also "strive for compromises." Grass concluded his Princeton address with the words: "Let us be conscious of this: A poem knows no compromises—but we live on compromises. He who actively sustains this tension is a fool and changes the world."

It is in the light of this that one must view Günter Grass's life and developing work since his move to Berlin, the erection of the wall on August 13, 1961, his open letter to Anna Seghers, and his coming out in support of the Social Democratic Party (in the pocket edition *Die Alternative* [The Alternative]) in August, 1961. Grass's temperament is such that even in the daily petty warfare of politics he remains the artist. He utilizes his "fool's freedom," as he does his growing fame, for agitation that often has a satiric tinge. This can be seen especially clearly in the "Rede über das Selbstverständliche" [Speech on the Self-evident], which he delivered on the occasion of his being awarded the Georg Büchner Prize in Darmstadt in October, 1965. In this speech, which gave some offense, he addressed himself to what he called "The motto-pulsing conscience of a nonexistent nation." It was no festival address—rather an election speech filled with ill-humor at the poor showing of the Social Democratic Party. If this speech is taken as the expression of a productive poet, and if it is read right after the novel *Dog Years,* it appears at times like a 104th Materniad. As a critic of the age he lives in and especially of the German mentality, Grass belongs to the line of succession that leads back through Heinrich Mann to Heinrich Heine. It would be easy for a historian, consulting facts and sifting sources, to make corrections, to point out that the comparisions, the proportions between the emigrant Büchner and the emigrant Willy Brandt do not tally. But as an autobiographic utterance and a polemic, this speech is of a high order.

In his essay "Der Inhalt als Widerstand" Grass had written:

The content is the inevitable resistance, the pretext for the form. One has form or feeling for form; one carries it about like a bomb in a valise, and all that is needed is the fuse —whether we call it story, fable, red thread, subject, or content—to conclude the long preparations for a great blast, a display of fireworks that unfolds at the right elevation, under favorable weather conditions, with the bang following a few seconds after the eye has had something to see.

In 1964 at the West Berlin Academy of Arts, Grass—who, as orator and essayist, writer of lyrics and epics, has a partiality for expressing himself dramatically—gave a formal address that had the baroque title "Vor- und Nachgeschichte der Tragödie des *Coriolanus* von Livius and Plutarch über Shakespeare bis zu Brecht und mir" [The Prehistory and Posthistory of the Tragedy of *Coriolanus,* from Livy and Plutarch via Shakespeare down to Brecht and Myself], in which he (as it were) "took a bomb from his valise" and showed how he would set the fuse for a theatrical "act of violence."

Grass spoke of Bertolt Brecht's having adapted (between 1952 and 1953) Shakespeare's *Coriolanus,* "this tragedy that is still virulent today." Grass continued:

During the time he was doing the adaptation came the fatal date, June 17. While Brecht, supported by Livy, racked his brains over how Shakespeare's plebeians, armed only with clubs, could be given greater ability to strike, the unarmed and unrehearsed construction workers of the Stalinallee rebelled in protest against the raising of the norms of production just as the plebeians had rebelled against the exorbitant grain prices. Here is occasion for a theater play that could be called *The Plebeians Rehearse the Uprising.* The place of action: a rehearsal stage in East Berlin. Someone who is referred to by his assistants and the actors as "the boss" is rehearsing the opening scene of *Coriolanus,* and wishes to keep this revolt from taking on something of the ridiculous and hopeless.

Here Grass added the comment that Brecht was, as a matter of fact, not rehearsing *Coriolanus* on June 17; in other words he separated the facts from his fiction, which fiction basically served as an exploration of reality—more exactly, as an analysis of the behavior of an intellectual in a situation requiring him to make a decision. Grass said:

In my play the construction workers petition the boss or theater director for a document with his important signature. They want him to frame, in words that they themselves cannot find, their awkward summons for a general strike which the American radio RIAS would neither edit nor broadcast. . . . In my play the theater director does not flatly refuse to write the text that the workers hope for. He intends to draft it as soon as the masons and carpenters have demonstrated to him how people behaved on the Stalinallee at the beginning of the uprising. For him the main thing is to utilize a current issue for his staging of *Coriolanus*, his plebeians' uprising.

In history—for the seventeenth of June has become history—and in my theater, Soviet tanks make the uprising collapse. While the workers in the theater play regard the attack of the tanks as fate, which they can at most oppose with stones or not oppose at all, the theater director holds an extemporaneous discourse on the subject of whether and how armored vehicles can be used on the stage. For him, whatever happens becomes a stage scene—slogans, spoken choruses, the question of whether to march in a column of tens or twelves, everything becomes an aesthetic question—his is an unmixed theatrical nature. The fun of the tragedy. Shakespeare's *Coriolanus* and the theater director's *Coriolanus*. Two tribunes of the people and two staff members of the Berlin Ensemble. Blind fate and controlled theatrical intent. Prices of grain and raising of norms. Revolts of plebeians, and of construction workers. A public square, and the seat of government at the corner of Leipziger Strasse. Livy, Plutarch, and the broadcasting regulations of RIAS. History and its treatment. Intellectual property and its possessors. The National Holiday and the Shakespeare year. This play has to be written.

The play was written. Grass took the "Vorläufige Fassung, März 1965" [Preliminary Version, March, 1965] with him to the United States, meaning to give it the finishing touches there. But on his return that summer he brought back with him, not the play ready for the stage, but two election campaign speeches in behalf of the Social Democratic Party—"Was ist des Deutschen Vaterland?" [What Is the German Fatherland?] and "Loblied auf Willy" [Panegyric on Willy]. Later he supplemented these with three additional speeches—"Es steht zur Wahl" [Here Is the Choice], "Des Kaisers neue Kleider [The Emperor's New Clothes], and "Ich klage an" [I Accuse]—and the "Speech on the Self-evident," which he delivered when he received the Büchner Prize. An echo of polemical rhetoric is also noticeable in some passages of *The Plebeians*. More important than this influence, however, was the experience of contact with the crowd and its reactions, often positive, sometimes turbulently protesting. These experiences stood Grass in good stead in the drafting of the final version of his play, which was finished only shortly before the first performance. The criticism of Brecht (the prototype of the theater director) became criticism of the behavior of the intellectual generally. Included in this criticism was self-examination on the part of the author.

These factors, which influence each other, were emphasized by Grass at a press conference held in Berlin on January 16, 1966, the day after the opening.

The problem facing the theater director in his play, said Grass, is a general problem for intellectuals (by which he means not just authors but also members of other professions). The discrepancy between theory and practice results, on the one hand, in utopian demands made on reality that reality cannot meet, and, on the other hand, the disdain of reality in utopia.

Both the theoretical man and the pragmatic or practical man are at fault in equal degree here. This really constitutes the theme of the play: the continuing switch to the opposite. The arguments of the workers, the arguments of the theater director are almost always right, and yet not quite right. Each side's tenacity contributes imperceptibly to its guilt.

"Obviously," Grass added, "this play is also a question addressed to the writer himself. . . ."

He supplemented this statement in a conversation with Jens Hoffman (published in *Christ und Welt* on February 11, 1966) in which he explained that he did not mean with his play to "emphasize any one tendency by apportioning the roles on the stage." Nor did he mean to voice through any particular character his own views regarding the seventeenth of June. "I question my own tendency—that is to say, my own idea regarding the seventeenth of June—along with the others."

It is through this problem that the dramatic point of attack and the dramatic pivot of *The Plebeians* are to be seen. The author hopes to shed light on the problem for others while trying to achieve enlightenment himself with the help of his work, with the help of the characters in his play as they make themselves autonomous. He therefore does not provide a true representation of Brecht and his "failure" on the seventeenth of June. (How Brecht conducted himself on that day is told by Erwin Leiser in the *Weltwoche* of February 11, 1966.) For his starting point Grass takes a fiction that approximates reality only in part. He projects into this fiction the aforementioned problem, which is his own problem and should be the problem of all Germans in a divided homeland, a split nation. And he works through once again, in a kind of series of experiments, the range of what can be said for and against the rulers in East Berlin and West Berlin, for and against the insurgent workers, for and against the leading class of intellectuals.

A well-grounded critical evaluation of the play must begin by recognizing this foundation. It must test the approach, must emphasize the difficulties that arise both from the central figure, the theater director, and from inadequate or unequally distributed stresses. These difficulties serve to explain excessive strains that occur in the "series of experiments," above all in the scene where the director is to be hanged. On the whole the play is, nevertheless, solidly worked out, both from the point of view of language and the construction of its scenes. In some passages contact between the lyricists Brecht and Grass is strongly and beautifully manifested. Whether the author of *The Plebeians* has found the "third way" in his "German tragedy" may remain a matter of dispute. It is indisputable that in a few poems in recent years he has attained the highest peaks of his creative achievement to date. Here, in a form that is artistically without compromise, are combined *engagement* and wit, power of language and originality. The sin against the Holy Ghost, experienced in early youth, appears in the last lines of the poem "Kleckerburg" and, in wonderful variation, in the verses of the closing scene of the third act of *The Plebeians.*

Chronology

1927: Günter Grass born on October 16 in Danzig.

1933–1944: Elementary school and high school in Danzig. Luftwaffe assistant. Reich Labor Service.

1944–1945: Soldier. April 20, 1945, wounded at Cottbus. Military hospital at Marienbad. American prisoner-of-war camp in Bavaria.

1946: Released from prisoner-of-war camp. Farm work in the Rhineland. Worker in a potash mine.

1947: Stonemason apprentice in Düsseldorf (with the firms of Goebel and Moog, makers of gravestones).

1948–1949: Student in the sculpture and painting class of the Kunstakademie in Düsseldorf (Professors S. Mages and O. Pankok).

1951: Italian journey as far as Palermo.

1952: Residence in France. Kunstakademie in Berlin (Professor K. Hartung).

1954: Marries the dancer Anna Margaretha Schwarz, of Lenzburg, Switzerland. Third Prize in a lyric poetry contest sponsored by the South German Radio Network.

1955: Journey to Spain.

1956: Exhibition in Stuttgart (Galerie Lutz und Meyer). *Die Vorzüge der Windhühner* [The Merits of Windfowl]. Move to Paris.

1957: Exhibition of plastic and graphic art in the Kunstamt Berlin-Tempelhof. Birth of the twins Franz and Raoul. First performance of *Hochwasser* [The Flood] (by the Frankfurt Studentenbühne) and of the ballet *Stoffreste* [Material Remnants] (in the Stadttheater Essen, with choreography by Marcel Luitpart).

1958: Scholarship granted by the Kulturkreis der deutschen Industrie. Prize awarded by the Gruppe 47. Journey to Poland. *Onkel, Onkel* [Mister, Mister] (first performed by the Städtische Bühnen of Cologne).

1959: Exhibition of graphic art in Bremen. The Bremen Senate denies Grass the literature prize, which an independent panel of judges had awarded him. The ballet *Fünf Köche* [Five Cooks], with choreography by Marcel Luitpart, performed in Aix-les-Bains and Bonn. Second journey to Poland. *Die Blechtrommel* [The Tin Drum]. *Beritten hin und zurück* [Mounted Going There and Coming Back], performed by the Frankfurt Studentenbühne and by the Theater 53 in Hamburg. *Noch zehn Minuten bis Buffalo* [Only Ten Minutes to Buffalo], performed at the Schillertheater in Berlin.

1960: Move to Berlin. *Gleisdreieck* [Railroad-track Triangle]. Berlin Critics' Prize.

1961: Birth of his daughter Laura. Open letter to Anna Seghers (on the 13th of August). *Katz und Maus* [Cat and Mouse].

1962: *Die bösen Köche* [The Wicked Cooks], staged by Walter Henn and performed at the Schiller-theater in Berlin. French literary prize ("Le Meilleur Livre Etranger").

1963: New version of *Hochwasser. Hundejahre* [Dog Years]. Member of the Akademie der Künste. *Die Ballerina* (pamphlet).

1964: *Goldmäulchen,* performed in the Workshop Theater, Munich. On the occasion of Shakespeare's four-hundredth anniversary, "Die Vor- und Nachgeschichte der Tragödie des *Coriolanus* von Livius und Plutarch über Shakespeare bis zu Brecht und mir" [The Prehistory and Posthistory of the Tragedy of *Coriolanus,* from Livy and Plutarch via Shakespeare down to Brecht and Myself].

1965: New version of *Onkel, Onkel.* Birth of Grass's son Bruno. Journeys to the United States. Honorary doctor's degree conferred by Kenyon College, Gambier, Ohio. Election campaign trips and speeches for the Social Democratic Party, fifty-two separate events. Five of these speeches have been published (in *Über das Selbstverständliche*): "Was ist des Deutschen Vaterland?" [What Is the German Fatherland?]; "Loblied auf Willy" [Panegyric on Willy]; "Es steht zur Wahl" [Here Is the Choice]; "Des Kaisers neue Kleider" [The Emperor's New Clothes]; "Ich klage an" [I Accuse]. Phonograph record of "Es steht zur Wahl." Büchner Prize for 1965. "Rede über das Selbstverständliche" [Speech on the Self-Evident].

1966: *Die Plebejer proben den Aufstand* [The Plebeians Rehearse the Uprising], staged by Hansjörg Utzerath and performed at the Schillertheater in Berlin. "Vom mangelnden Selbstvertrauen der schreibenden Hofnarren unter Berücksichtigung nicht vorhandener Höfe" [On the Lack of Self-confidence of the Literary Court Jester Without a Court]. "Sechs Gedichte" [Six Poems] (published in *Akzente*).

Bibliography

Compiled by W. V. Blomster

Works by Günter Grass

NARRATIVE PROSE

Die Blechtrommel. Neuwied: Luchterhand, 1959.
> ENGLISH. *The Tin Drum,* trans. Ralph Manheim. New York: Pantheon, 1961. (Paper eds., Vintage and Fawcett.)

Katz und Maus. Neuwied: Luchterhand, 1961.
> ENGLISH. *Cat and Mouse,* trans. Ralph Manheim. New York: Harcourt, Brace and World, 1963. (Paper ed., Signet.)

Hundejahre. Neuwied: Luchterhand, 1963.
> ENGLISH. *Cat and Mouse,* trans. Ralph Manheim. York: Harcourt, Brace and World, 1965. (Paper ed., Fawcett.)

DRAMATIC WORKS

Noch zehn Minuten bis Buffalo. In *Deutsches Theater der Gegenwart,* Vol. I. Frankfurt: Suhrkamp, 1967. (Written in 1959; first published in *Akzente,* Vol. I, 1959.)

Hochwasser. Frankfurt: Edition Suhrkamp, 1963. (Written in 1955; revised in 1963.) A school edition of *Noch zehn Minuten bis Buffalo* and *Hochwasser,* edited and with an introduction by A. Leslie Willson, was published by Appleton-Century-Crofts, 1967.

Onkel, Onkel. Berlin: Wagenbach, 1965. (Written in 1956–57 and revised for publication in Wagenbach's *Quarthefte*.) Illustrated with nine drawings by Grass.

Die bösen Köche. In *Modernes Deutsches Theater,* Vol. I. Neuwied: Luchterhand, 1961. (Written in 1957.)

ENGLISH. Translations of these four dramas were published in *Four Plays* (New York: Harcourt, Brace and World, 1967; paperback ed.—A Harvest Book—also published by Harcourt, Brace and World). English titles are *Only Ten Minutes to Buffalo; Flood; Mister, Mister;* and *The Wicked Cooks*. First three plays translated by Ralph Manheim; *The Wicked Cooks,* by A. Leslie Willson. Introduction by Martin Esslin. Translation of *The Wicked Cooks* by James L. Rosenberg is included in *The New Theater of Europe,* Vol. II, ed. Robert W. Corrigan (New York: Dell, 1964). *Noch zehn Minuten bis Buffalo* appeared in a translation that evokes the figure of Casey Jones to preserve the railroad idiom—*The Salt Lake Line,* prepared by Christopher Holme. In *German Writing Today,* ed. Christopher Middleton (Baltimore: Penguin Books, 1967).

Die Plebejer proben den Aufstand: ein deutsches Trauerspiel. Neuwied: Luchterhand, 1966.

ENGLISH. *The Plebeians Rehearse the Uprising: A German Tragedy,* trans. Ralph Manheim. Includes Grass's address "The Prehistory and Posthistory of the Tragedy of *Coriolanus,* from Livy and Plutarch via Shakespeare down to Brecht and Myself," and documentary report, "The Uprising of June 17, 1953," by Uta Gerhardt. New York: Harcourt, Brace and World, 1966. The paperback edition—A Harvest Book—by Harcourt, Brace and World contains only the translated drama.

POETRY

Die Vorzüge der Windhühner. Neuwied: Luchterhand, 1956. 2d ed. 1963. Illustrated by Grass. Second edition includes more illustrations.

Gleisdreieck. Neuwied: Luchterhand, 1960. Illustrated with 18 drawings by Grass.

ENGLISH. *Selected Poems,* in German, with translations by Michael Hamburger and Christopher Middleton. London: Secker and Warburg, 1966. This volume contains 14 of the 40 poems published in *Die Vorzüge der Windhühner* and 14 of the 56 poems contained in *Gleisdreieck.*

Ausgefragt. Neuwied: Luchterhand, 1967. Illustrated by Grass.

ENGLISH. *New Poems,* in German, with translations by Michael Hamburger. New York: Harcourt, Brace and World, 1968. Of the 60 poems in *Ausgefragt,* 27 are published in this volume.

POLITICAL AND CRITICAL WRITINGS

Über das Selbstverständliche: Reden, Aufsätze, Offene Briefe, Kommentare. Neuwied: Luchterhand, 1968.

ENGLISH. *Speak Out!: Speeches, Open Letters, Commentaries,* trans. Ralph Manheim and others. New York: Harcourt, Brace and World, 1969. A selection from *Über das Selbstverständliche* and other sources.

Briefe über die Grenze. With Pavel Kohout. Hamburg: Wegner, 1968. An exchange of letters between Grass and the Czech writer and theatrical producer Kohout on the position of the artist in the Eastern state. Grass's letter to the former Czech President Anthonin Novotny of September 5, 1967, is also included.

Tschechoslowakei 1968. Zurich: Verlag der Arche, 1968. Speeches delivered in the Stadttheater Basel on September 8, 1968, by Grass, Peter Bichsel, Friedrich Dürrenmatt, Max Frisch, and Kurt Marti. A letter by Heinrich Böll, read at that time, is also included.

Über meinen Lehrer Döblin und andere Vorträge. Berlin: Literarisches Colloquium, 1968.

Secondary Literature and Critical Reviews

Anon. "Drum of Neutrality." *The Times Literary Supplement,* (October 5, 1962), 776.

Anon. "Grass Takes to the Stump." *America,* 113 (July 24, 1965), 89.

Anon. "Leaves of Grass." *Time* (April 1, 1966).

Anon. "The Plebeians Rehearse the Uprising." *Nation,* 204 (February 13, 1967).

Anon. "The Plebeians Rehearse the Uprising." *Life,* 60 (February 18, 1966), 17.

Ahl, Herbert. "Ohne Scham—ohne Tendenz—ohne Devise: Günter Grass." *Literarische Porträts* (Munich, 1962–1964), 28–35.

Andrews, R. C. "The Tin Drum." *Modern Languages,* 45:1 (1964), 28–31.

Ascherson, Neal. Review of *Dog Years. New Statesman,* 70 (November 26, 1965), 843.

——. Review of *The Tin Drum. New Statesman,* 64 (September 28, 1962), 62.

Atkinson, Brooks. Review of *The Plebeians Rehearse the Uprising. Saturday Review,* 49 (December 31, 1966), 26.

Augstein, Rudolf. "William Shakespeare, Bertolt Brecht, Günter Grass." *Der Spiegel* (January 24, 1966).

Barrett, William. Review of *Cat and Mouse. Atlantic,* 212 (September 1963), 122.

——. Review of *The Tin Drum. Atlantic,* 211 (May 1963), 132.

Bauke, Joseph. Review of *Cat and Mouse. Saturday Review,* 46 (August 10, 1963), 28.

——. Review of *Cat and Mouse. Time,* 82 (August 23, 1963), 75.

——. Review of *Cat and Mouse. The Times Literary Supplement* (September 27, 1963), 728.

Burns, R. K. Review of *Cat and Mouse,* by Günter Grass. *Library Journal,* 88 (August 1963), 2926.

——. Review of *Dog Years. Library Journal,* 90 (June 1965), 2582.

——. Review of *The Tin Drum. Library Journal,* 88 (February 15, 1963), 794.

Calisher, Hortense. Review of *The Tin Drum. Nation,* 196 (March 16, 1963), 229.

Carey, John. Review of *Selected Poems. New Statesman,* 71 (February 18, 1966), 232.

Clements, R. J. Review of *Selected Poems. Saturday Review,* 49 (May 21, 1966), 30.

Cunliffe, W. G. "Aspects of the Absurd in Günter Grass." *Wisconsin Studies in Contemporary Literature,* 7:3 (Autumn 1966), 311–327.

Cunliffe, W. G. "Günter Grass: *Katz und Maus.*" *Studies in Short Fiction,* 2:2 (Winter 1966), 174–185.

Davenport, Guy. Review of *Cat and Mouse. National Review,* 15 (October 8, 1963), 313.

——. Review of *Dog Years. National Review,* 17 (July 27, 1965), 659.

——. Review of *The Tin Drum. National Review,* 14 (April 9, 1963), 287.

Deen, R. F. Review of *Selected Poems. Commonweal,* 84 (September 16, 1966), 594.

Enright, D. J. Review of *Cat and Mouse. New Statesman,* 66 (August 23, 1963), 227.

——. Review of *Dog Years. New York Review of Books,* 4 (June 3, 1965), 8.

——. Review of *Selected Poems. New York Review of Books,* 7 (December 29, 1966), 7.

——. Review of *The Plebeians Rehearse the Uprising. New York Review of Books,* 7 (December 29, 1966), 7.

Enzensberger, Hans Magnus. "Trommelt weiter." *Frankfurter Hefte* (December 1961).

——. Günter Grass: "Hundejahre." *Der Spiegel* (September 4, 1963).

Ewen, Frederic. Review of *The Plebeians Rehearse the Uprising. Nation,* 204 (February 13, 1967), 213.

Fehse, Willi. *Von Goethe bis Grass: Biografische Porträts zur Literatur* (Bielefeld, 1963).

Fischer, Heinz. "Sprachliche Tendenzen bei Heinrich Böll und Günter Grass." *German Quarterly,* 40, 372–383.

Friedrichsmeyer, E. M. "Aspects of Myth, Parody and Obscenity in Günter Grass's *Die Blechtrommel* and *Katz und Maus.*" *The Germanic Review,* 40:3 (1965), 240–250.

Gaus, Günter. *Zur Person: Porträts in Frage und Antwort,* Vol. 2 (Munich, 1966).

Gregory, Horace. Review of *The Tin Drum. Common-
    weal,* 78 (April 26, 1963), 147.

Gregory, Sister M. Review of *Four Plays. Best Seller,*
    27 (April 15, 1967), 37.

Grumbach, Doris. Review of *The Tin Drum. Critic,* 21
    (June 1963), 81.

Hatfield, Henry. "Günter Grass: The Artist as Satirist."
    The Contemporary Novel in Germany (Austin:
    University of Texas, 1967), 115–134.

Hohoff, Curt. "Die Welt der Vogelscheuchen." *Rhein-
    ischer Merkur* (November 15, 1963).

Holthusen, Hans Egon. "Günter Grass als politischer
    Autor." *Der Monat,* 18:216 (September 1966),
    66–81.

Ivey, Frederick M. *"The Tin Drum* or Retreat to the
    Word." *Wichita State University Bulletin,* 40
    (February 1966).

Jens, Walter. "Das Pandämonium des Günter Grass."
    Die Zeit, 18:36 (1963), 17.

Jerde, C. D. "A Corridor of Pathos: Notes on the Fic-
    tion of Günter Grass." *Minnesota Review,* 4:4
    (Summer 1964) 558–560.

Kahler, Erich. "Form und Entformung." *Merkur,* 19
    (1965), 318–335, 413–428.

Kluger, Richard. "Tumultuous Indictment of Man."
    Harper's, 230 (June 1965), 110 ff.

Knight, Max. Review of *Selected Poems,* by Günter
    Grass. *New York Times Book Review,* (August
    14, 1966), 5.

Kohout, Pavel. "A Reply to Günter Grass." *Atlas* (No-
    vember 1967), 55–57.

Kunkel, Francis L. "Clowns and Saviours: Two Con-
    temporary Novels." *Renascence,* 18:1 (Fall
    1965), 40–44.

Lindley, Denver. Review of *The Tin Drum. New York
    Herald Tribune* (April 7, 1963), 1.

Lindroth, J. R. Review of *Dog Years. America,* 112 (June 26, 1965), 903.

Loschütz, Gert, ed. *Von Buch zu Buch: Günter Grass in der Kritik* (Neuwied: Luchterhand, 1968). This volume, subtitled "Eine Dokumentation," contains fifty-six articles on Grass and his works. They are, for the most part, reviews which were published immediately after the appearance of individual works by Grass. An extensive bibliography of criticism is included. The collection itself and the bibliography are restricted to publications from the German-speaking countries.

McDonnel, T. P. Review of *Dog Years. Critic* (June 1965), 24.

McGovern, Hugh. Review of *Cat and Mouse. America,* 109 (September 14, 1963), 264.

——. Review of *The Tin Drum. America,* 108 (March 9, 1963), 344.

Maddocks, Melvin. Review of *Dog Years. Christian Science Monitor* (May 27, 1965), 7.

Maloff, Saul. Review of *Dog Years. Commonweal,* 83 (December 3, 1965), 287.

Mander, John. Review of *Four Plays. Book Week* (May 21, 1967), 12.

Marcus, Klein. Review of *Dog Years. Reporter,* 33 (August 12, 1965), 51.

Maurer, Robert. "The End of Innocence: Günter Grass's *The Tin Drum.*" *Bucknell Review,* 16:2 (1968), 45–65.

Mayer-Amery, C. "Gruppe 47 at Princeton." *Nation,* 202 (May 16, 1966), 588–590.

Morton, Frederic. Review of *The Tin Drum. New York Times Book Review* (April 7, 1963), 5.

Murray, J. G. Review of *Cat and Mouse. Critic,* 22 (October 1963), 77.

Nonnenmann, Klaus, ed. *Schriftsteller der Gegenwart* (Olten and Freiburg, 1963).

Parry, Idris. "Aspects of Günter Grass's Narrative Technique." *Forum for Modern Language Studies* 3, 100–114.

Peters, H. F. Review of *Dog Years*. *Saturday Review,* 48 (May 29, 1965), 25.

——. Review of *Dog Years*. *Time,* 85 (May 28, 1965), 110.

——. Review of *Dog Years*. *Times Literary Supplement* (November 11, 1965), 997.

Pisko, E. S. Review of *The Tin Drum*. *Christian Science Monitor* (March 7, 1963), 10.

Plant, Richard. Review of *The Tin Drum*. *Times Literary Supplement* (October 5, 1962), 776.

——. Review of *The Tin Drum*. *Saturday Review,* 46 (March 9, 1963), 35.

Plard, Henri. "Verteidigung der Blechtrommeln." *Text und Kritik,* 1 (1965), 18.

Quinn, J. J. Review of *Cat and Mouse*. *Best Seller,* 23 (August 15, 1963), 162.

——. Review of *Cat and Mouse*. *Christian Century,* 80 (August 7, 1963), 983.

——. Review of *The Tin Drum*. *Best Seller,* 23 (April 1963), 12.

Rachow, L. A. Review of *Four Plays*. *Library Journal,* 92 (April 1, 1967), 1508.

——. Review of *The Plebeians Rehearse the Uprising*. *Library Journal,* 91 (November 15, 1966), 5641.

Reich-Ranicki, Marcel. "Günter Grass, unser grimmiger Idylliker." *Deutsche Literatur in West und Ost* (Munich: Piper, 1963), 216–230.

Roloff, M. "Günter Grass." *Atlantic,* 215 (June 1965), 94–97.

Roloff, M. Review of *The Plebeians Rehearse the Up-rising. Commonweal,* 86 (May 19, 1967), 266.

Rovit, Earl. Review of *Dog Years. American Scholar,* 34 (Autumn 1965), 676.

Ruhleder, Karl H. "A Pattern of Messianic Thought in Günter Grass' Cat and Mouse." *German Quarterly,* 39:4 (November 1966), 599–612.

Scherman, D. E. "Green Years for Grass." *Life,* 58 (June 4, 1965), 51–52.

Schlocker, Georges. "Une piece de Günter Grass." *Lettres Nouvelles* (March-April 1966), 136–139.

Schott, Webster. Review of *The Plebeians Rehearse the Uprising. New York Times Book Review,* 20 (1966), 4.

Sharfman, William L. "The Organization of Experience in *The Tin Drum." Minnesota Review,* 6:1 (1966), 59–65.

Simon, John. Review of *Dog Years. Book Week,* (May 23, 1965), 1.

Solotaroff, Theodore. Review of *Dog Years. New Republic,* 152 (June 19, 1965), 21.

Spender, Stephen. Review of *Cat and Mouse. Newsweek,* 62 (September 9, 1963), 93.

———. Review of *Cat and Mouse. New Yorker,* 39 (August 10, 1963), 88.

———. Review of *Cat and Mouse. New York Times Book Review* (August 11, 1963), 5.

———. "Scarecrows and Swastikas." (Review of *Dog Years). The New York Times Book Review,* (May 23, 1965).

Steiner, George. "The Nerve of Günter Grass." *Commentary,* 37:5 (May 1964), 77–80.

Subiotto, Arrigo. "Günter Grass." *Essays on Contemporary German Literature* (ed. Brian Keith-Smith), *German Men of Letters, 4* (London, 1966).

Sutton, Ellen. "Grass and Bobrowski." *Times Literary Supplement* (February 17, 1966), 123.

Verleihung des Georg-Büchner-Preises 1965 an Günter Grass. Festrede von Ernst Schütte. Laudatio von Kasimir Edschmid. (Neuwied: Luchterhand, 1965.)

Wagenbach, Klaus. "Günter Grass." *Deutsche Literatur der Gegenwart* (Olten: Walter, 1963), 118 ff.

West, Anthony. Review of *Dog Years. Newsweek,* 65 (May 24, 1965), 116.

——. Review of *Dog Years. New Yorker,* 41 (November 20, 1965), 236.

Wieser, Theodor. *Günter Grass* (Neuwied: Luchterhand, 1968). In the series "Porträt und Poesie." In addition to a lengthy introductory essay by Wieser the volume contains an extensive selection from the poetry of Grass along with several brief prose compositions.

Willson, A. Leslie. "The Grotesque Everyman in Günter Grass's *Die Blechtrommel.*" *Monatshefte,* 18:2 (Summer 1966), 131–138.

Yates, Norris W. *Günter Grass, A Critical Essay* (Grand Rapids: W. B. Eerdmans, 1967).

Zimmermann, Werner. "Von Ernst Wiechert zu Günter Grass." *Wirkendes Wort,* 15:5 (1965), 316–326.

Zwerenz, Gerhard. "Brecht, Grass und der 17. Juni, 11 Anmerkungen." *Theater heute* (July 1966.)